42 Rules for Your New Leadership Role

The Manual They Didn't Hand You When You Made VP, Director, or Manager

By Pam Fox Rollin

Foreword by John A. Byrne
Editor-in-Chief, Poets&Quants
Former Executive Editor,
BusinessWeek and *Fast Company*

ſUPeRſtaR
press

E-mail: info@superstarpress.com
20660 Stevens Creek Blvd., Suite 210
Cupertino, CA 95014

Published by Super Star Press™, a Happy About® imprint
20660 Stevens Creek Blvd., Suite 210, Cupertino, CA 95014
http://42rules.com

First Printing: April 2011
Paperback ISBN: 978-1-60773-034-7 (1-60773-034-0)
eBook ISBN: 978-1-60773-035-4 (1-60773-035-9)
Place of Publication: Silicon Valley, California, USA
Library of Congress Number: 2011902588

Trademarks

Warning and Disclaimer

Praise For This Book!

"I wish I had this book early in my career! By now, I've seen hundreds of people start leadership roles—from senior executives to customer-facing team leads—some starting brilliantly, some struggling unnecessarily. This book points you to the actions that make all the difference in those critical early months."
Peter Aceto, CEO, ING DIRECT, Canada

"This book will be useful when you start and as a framework throughout your career as you take on ever more challenging roles. You'll especially value, as I do, Pam's perspective on building the relationships and fact base that make extraordinary work possible."
Steven Tallman, Partner & VP, Global Operations, Bain & Company

"Pam and I met 10 years ago when we started our coaching company. Since inception Pam has been one of our most effective and loved coaches. Her clients love her because of how she helps them reach the heights they were capable of. 42 Rules for Your New Leadership Role *represents the best of what she has learned over the years. Buy this book, and expect it to change your life!"*
Scott Blanchard, Executive Vice President, The Ken Blanchard Companies

"When I mentor leaders who want to advance, I offer the guidance you'll find in this book: Be bold in seeing opportunities and tackling tough issues, build your visibility strategically, and take responsibility for your own development. I've heard Pam speak on this, and she gives you the real scoop."
Genevieve Haldeman, Vice President, Corporate Communications, Symantec

"Leaders thrive on making bold moves amid risk. At the same time, the best stay open to learning. Let Pam help you raise your game on both fronts."
Steve Jurvetson, Managing Director, Draper Fisher Jurvetson

"Pam was a key partner in transforming my team from a sales support organization to one providing strategic marketing leadership. With her warm and direct style, Pam assisted me in tackling the challenges of being new to the company, new to the industry, and new to leadership level. With my reports (many of whom were also new), Pam developed their leadership skills, strategic thinking, and implementation planning. The wisdom in this slim, yet impactful, book provides new leaders a road map to success."
Gail Piccirilli, former VP Marketing, Blue Shield of California

"Leadership transitions lay the groundwork for more great legacies and painful failures than any other period in your career. Don't let past success fool you into thinking you can wing it. Use a set of practical steps, like these wisely crafted rules, to help you quickly identify blind spots, build allies, and set norms that will assure you (and your team!) get to the next stage."
Mike Hochleutner, Executive Director, Center for Leadership Development and Research, Stanford Graduate School of Business

"Pam gives us that rare gem of a book—the perfect blend of proven tactics solidly grounded in the latest research. 42 Rules for Your New Leadership Role *offers smart, busy leaders the proven mindsets and practical to-do's to make their strongest start as they rise in the leadership ranks. She also provides great tips on leading change across your organization. Refer back to the book often, and take every chance to hear Pam speak about leadership."*
Sharon L. Richmond, Director, Change Leadership Center of Excellence, Cisco Systems

"Winning markets is always a combination of a brilliant idea, created in collaboration with people. It is always a combination of the 'what' and the 'how.' Many books will offer you frameworks and models. This book will give you pure wisdom on 'how' you can lead, so you and your company can win."
Nilofer Merchant, Strategist and Author of *The New How*

"Pam Fox Rollin and her new book give even the most junior leaders advice that can make them 'wise' beyond their years. Take a look at her criteria for a win/win project:

- *Makes a real impact on the P&L*
- *Seen as a win by people with power*
- *Relieves a significant pain for your team*
- *Can be replicated, rolled out, or scaled up*
- *Engages a cross-section of people on your team*
- *Generates learning that makes your team more capable of future wins.*

I do not think any consultant could give you better advice. Read her. Follow her. Succeed because of her."
Linda Alepin, Dean's Executive Professor of Entrepreneurship, Santa Clara University and Founding Director, Global Women's Leadership Network

"42 Rules for Your New Leadership Role covers all the critical first steps to take and all the dangerous missteps to avoid as you dive into a new role, a new company, and a new culture. Pam's insight into what it takes to not only get off on the right foot but to rise in the best technology-driven companies makes this book relevant in Silicon Valley and around the world."
Mark Roe, Vice President of Operations, SolarCity and former executive, Apple

"I work with people who are reinventing their careers, and one of their biggest fears is whether or not they'll be effective in their new jobs. They're especially concerned about taking on a new leadership role. Pam has created an easy-to-follow set of guidelines that lay out the key issues leaders need to think about so that they can feel confident right from the start. Brilliant!"
Dr. Susan Bernstein, Career Reinvention & Renewal Coach, Work from Within

"When making the transition to a new role, even a top performer needs to exercise a different group of muscles. Pam has distilled extensive leadership lessons into simple and actionable guidelines. With the insights from this book, you can make your next start your best ever."
Judy Gilbert, Director of People Operations, YouTube

Dedication

This book is dedicated to the amazing leaders at Bain & Company and Accenture who mentored me through those first few months and many more.

Acknowledgments

I wanted this book to be fast to read, so you—incredibly busy with a new job—can gain insights and tactics quickly.

What I know now is that "fast to read" does not mean "fast to write." The editor of the *42 Rules* series, Laura Lowell, is the soul of patient persistence; hence, you have this book today. She is also quite fluent with Track Changes, to your benefit and mine.

Many thanks to each of the executives—named and anonymous—who shared their experiences for this book.

My work is deeply informed by my colleagues from what became the Center for Leadership Development & Research at Stanford University's Graduate School of Business. I am especially grateful for conversations with Ed Batista, Beth Benjamin, Mary Ann Huckabay, and Evelyn Williams. Former and current Stanford GSB faculty David Bradford, Deborah Gruenfeld, Kirk Hansen, Rod Kramer, Jim March, Joanne Martin, Debra Meyerson, Margaret Neale, Charles O'Reilly, Jeffrey Pfeffer, Joel Podolny, Bob Sutton, and Jim Thompson have influenced my thinking.

I am ever grateful to my consulting "brain trust": Lilia Shirman (author of *42 Rules for Growing Enterprise Revenue*), Robbie Baxter, Niti Agrawal, and Steph Cipresse. I am likewise appreciative of mentors and friends from my work in strategy consulting and nonprofit leadership—they knew I had a book in me, and they've stayed in touch long enough to see it.

Dario Nardi, Katherine Hirsh, Linda Berens, Jane Kise, Kris Kiler, Sharon Richmond, Julie Brown, and Wendy Appel have shaped my perspective on personality type and leadership as we've shared podiums, research projects, and late nights at conference bars.

Peter Mello, founder and co-host of our Weekly Leader podcast, makes learning leadership fun and accessible. I look forward each week to our recording sessions.

Valued colleagues Andrea Bauer, Fran Sachs, Bart Fisher, Judith Wilson, plus English teacher Ann Fox (aka Mom) read early drafts and improved all they saw. Thanks as well to my amazing assistant, Jennifer Doolin, who tracked down the last details.

My husband Keith now has a fellow author in the family, though he warned me "you don't make money writing books."

True...yet books do change lives. Other authors have done this for me. I am honored that through this book you've given me the chance to contribute to your next success.

Contents

Foreword by John A. Byrne

Recently, I reviewed on Poets&Quants the first 100 days of Kellogg business school's new dean. An alum, Sally Blount came back after 22 years...with a minimal internal network and no mandate for change. What she does have is huge energy, a track record of exceeding fundraising and academic metrics, the smarts to learn from others, and understanding how essential that is in Kellogg's collaborative culture.

In those important first months, she traveled and met near-constantly with hundreds of alums, faculty, and students, asked the big questions, and listened intently. She also knocked out 18 blog posts to reduce the mystery of what she was up to, demonstrate she was hearing stakeholders, and point attention toward significant aspects of Kellogg's brand and potential as she lay the groundwork for creating more specific strategic initiatives. Her goals were to become known rapidly to the Kellogg community and to build support for tackling together Kellogg's toughest issues. By all accounts, she hit those goals. This gives her even more credibility and momentum for the hard work ahead.

How will your first 100 days stack up to hers?

Drawing on the vast literature of leadership, Pam Fox Rollin has given us a superb primer on starting successfully. She tees up tactics and mindsets for executives and managers who have just assumed a new leadership role—how to leverage your inevitable honeymoon period (they rarely last long), how to engage your team members (some of whom wanted your job), and how to spread responsibility instead of blame. She tells us how to pick smart quick wins (yes, first impressions still count heavily) and how to set realistic milestones.

You'll find the essentials—"what" and "how"—are skillfully captured in this book. Use it to guide your start, and you'll have the advantage of Pam's experience as confidential coach to senior executives and top MBAs. What you have to bring is the "why," something that no author can offer. It's up to you to bring an honest heart, intense commitment, empathy for your team, and ambition for the organization, as well as yourself.

Lately, I've been spending time with a champion leader, someone who built a $4 billion dollar company from scratch. In the process, he became a billionaire. So did his two brothers. And more than 50 members of the team that helped to make this possible became millionaires. This was no sexy dot-com. It was a company that started as an auto parts distributor in Cleveland.

For all of his life, he thought climbing the mountain meant success in business and in the philanthropic world where he has long been heavily involved. His search for meaning, instead, ends with a mirror. When he looks into it every morning, he likes who he sees. He is proud of the person he sees. He respects himself. At the end of the day, I believe this is the essence of leadership.

Take the excellent guidance in this book. And, search your heart and soul for the integrity and commitment that will inspire you and your organization. Choose to be a leader of consequence. Only you can do that.

John A. Byrne
Editor-in-Chief, Poets&Quants
Former Executive Editor, *BusinessWeek* **and** *Fast Company*

My first day of my first post-college job, as an Associate Consultant at Bain & Company, a guy a year ahead of me responded to my first voicemail as follows: "Pam, I didn't listen to your whole message, and neither will anyone else here. If you want people to listen, start this way: 'I'm calling for two pieces of data and to ask you to introduce me to Joe. The data I need are X and Y. I want you to introduce me to Joe this week so I can talk with him about Z.' Try it again." Felt like a punch in the gut at the time, but soon I realized the favor he did me. I tightened up my communication and became more effective.

When you started an entry-level job, you probably got lots of feedback and suggestions for how to do better. Front-line managers and experienced colleagues are generally willing to tell "the new kid" what works around here and what doesn't.

Now that you're stepping up to a new leadership role, you're far less likely to receive useful guidance. This holds true whether you are in your first manager role or an experienced leader joining top executive ranks. I find this problem is especially acute for new Directors and VPs. You've been hired at these levels for your track record, so people assume you know what to do.

However, just because you were successful in your last role doing or managing marketing, accounting, engineering, or whatever you did, doesn't mean you know how to make a strong start at your next job. You could use some guidance—or reminders, at least—on how to make those critical first weeks successful.

I wrote *42 Rules for Your New Leadership Role* to fill that gap.

What you'll find in this book

Based on two decades of coaching senior leaders, helping executive teams craft strategy, and guiding Stanford MBAs, I describe a proven set of approaches to teach you what you've yet to learn, remind you of what you already know, and inspire you to become the best leader you can be in this job...and your next...and your next.

You can also use these rules to coach your team members to their highest performance. Often, it's hard for people who do something well (such as leading) to reflect on what they do and break it down so they can teach it to others. Let this book help you grow the leadership strength of your team and earn your reputation as a great boss and mentor.

To make this book even more useful for you, I've created an ever-expanding set of downloadable worksheets, free to readers of this book (http://ideashape.com/leadstartbook/resources). You will find frameworks and tips to support your leadership success.

Let's get started...

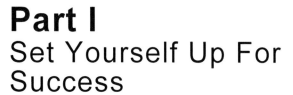

Part I
Set Yourself Up For Success

Congratulations on stepping up your leadership!

To ready yourself for the intense months ahead, scale up your task management system so you can meet commitments flawlessly.

Put your head into the game. Make sure you're familiar with major strategic issues facing your industry, company, and group.

Think through the fact base and people you'll need to know to make a great start. Draft your own onboarding plan, in addition to any official onboarding process from your company.

If you've already started, skim these Rules to see if there are steps you missed and want to handle right away.

- Rule 1: Rules Are Meant To Be Broken
- Rule 2: Begin Ready
- Rule 3: Fire Up Your Task Management System
- Rule 4: Draft Your Strategic One-Pager
- Rule 5: Take Charge of Your Start

1

Rules Are Meant to Be Broken

"Welcome to your new leadership role: You have a bigger job in a tough climate with very little support!"

That's why you want to lead, right? You want to forge your own path and make your own rules! You're on fire to wow your customers, astonish the market, and create wins for you and your team.

You've probably noticed that some ways of leading tend to work better than others. Take sole credit for a team win? Bad. Engage your team in figuring out how you'll make the numbers? Good.

Leaders at all levels succeed or fail for a surprisingly common set of reasons: meeting business objectives, succeeding in interpersonal relationships, building a great team, and adapting to change.[1]

These reasons hold true across industries, time, and market conditions.

One-quarter of senior executives promoted from within fail in the first 18 months; one-third of outside hires fail.[2] Many flame-outs can be traced to missteps during their first quarter. More importantly, for the 60–75 percent of leaders who survive into the second year, their effectiveness and trajectory are powerfully affected by choices made as they start.

---

1. Ellen Van Velsor and Jean Brittain, "Why Executives Derail," *Academy of Management Executive 9*, no. 4 (1995): 62–72.
2. L. Kelly-Radford, "The Revolving Door of Talent," *CEO Magazine*, August/September, 2001, 86–89.

Why is this so hard?

If you're like the technology leaders, marketing executives, and top teams I coach, you might notice how easy it is to become so caught up in fighting fires that you forget to shut off the gas. Or, you suspect you're lousy at certain aspects of leadership, so you ignore them and hope they won't bite you.

Or, maybe you never learned the rules in the first place! Leadership is an apprenticeship craft. One by-product of the dot-com boom and mid-2000s boom is that many of today's leaders are people who were rapidly promoted during boom years—and many of them were moving too fast with too little adult supervision to learn how to lead well.

With the trend toward more "flat" organizations, your boss may be stretched so thin that he/she can barely advocate for your team, let alone mentor you. Welcome to your new leadership role—you have a bigger job, in a tough climate, with very little support!

Learn the rules, then bend or break them

As you read this book, take what I say as a starting point for your own good thinking. Adjust what you find here to serve your team's needs, the market conditions, the cultural context, your goals, and your personal leadership approach.

The intense learning curve and unfamiliar environments of a new job make it difficult for your brain to consider options and make decisions as well as you usually do. When brains are overloaded, people tend to rely on what they've done before, even when that didn't work very well or is out of place in the new context. Ironically, this tunnel vision and rigidity is especially true of leaders who have experienced success—people like you who have been promoted or recruited for a new role.

So use this book to prompt what you might want to do at each phase of your start. Ask yourself what from this material will be useful to you in the week ahead. Then, ask yourself what's missing, what you want to do differently, and which rules you'll break entirely. See what results you're getting, and come back to this process at the end of the week.

Consider the rules, make up your own mind, act, observe, and reflect. Repeat. Succeed.

2 Begin Ready

"Shake off your old job (or job hunt), and start the new one rested."

They want you to start on Monday. Don't. Get your act together first.

Think more deeply

You researched before you began to interview. You scoured the company site, blogs, and news releases for clues on strategy and culture. You pumped your network for information.

Now it's time to inquire more deeply, to change your question from "Do I want to work for this company?" to "How can I thrive as a leader in this company?" and "What does my team need to do to succeed?

Michael Thompson, a serial senior executive highly respected by investors, writes his 120-day plan before he starts. His plan makes a handy discussion-starter for that final interview with the CEO.

Build relationships before you start

From Offer Day to Start Day, never have coffee alone. Engage with people in your new world as early as possible. (See Rule #6 for guidance on these conversations.)

C-level recruiter Ben Anderson of Lonergan Partners points out that external candidates often have more extensive and direct conversations with company leaders throughout the recruiting process. As an outsider, they are able to challenge leadership on the business, markets, products and people. Internal candidates often start new jobs at a disadvantage, never having talked with their new bosses and peers about their perspectives on the business and expectations from this role.

When one of my interviewees was promoted to VP of Engineering at a global software company, he headed to the airport to go see his former peers in several countries—before the promotion announcement. He spent a day 1:1 with each key team member at a comfortable spot out of the office, sharing his thoughts about where to take the company, gaining input, and helping each see a positive future with his leadership. Those conversations kept his former peers on the team, rather than rushing to LinkedIn to update their profiles.

Freshen up

What do you absolutely need to clean up before you start? Your car? Your calendar? Your relationship? If you've got a personal issue to solve in the next three months, see if you can get it 80% handled before you start.

Consider taking a "reset" vacation. Shake off the old job (or job hunt) and start the new one rested. For you, is this a weekend out in nature, a week of sleep at home, or a month of exotic travel? Do not roll from your current exhaustion right to your new job.

Make agreements with your loved ones

Becoming effective in your new position will require substantial mental energy and time, especially the first few months.

If you have a close partner, ask his or her thoughts on your start date —whether it's more important to take that long-deferred vacation or to go on payroll and health insurance ASAP. Figure out together if your family needs extra help—meals delivered, relocation assistance, an errand service. Talk about how you can keep your relationship warm and fun, though you'll have less time.

Make firm commitments to do the top things that keep you healthy and sane, such as working out, eating well, play time with your kids, sleeping at least seven hours.

Negotiate your start date

Given the business reconnaissance you plan to do, the rest you need, and any family considerations, when do you want to start? If you want a later start date than they request, make sure to negotiate in a manner that represents you well. Be eager to start, yet wise about starting well; considerate, but not spineless; collaborative, rather than adversarial. Let your tone suit the culture and your own leadership style.

3 Fire Up Your Task Management System

"Better to have an imperfect solution you use all the time, than an elegant solution you use half the time."

There's no substitute for being organized.

For baseline credibility, you must manage yourself to

- Show up on time, prepared to use other people's time well
- Determine dates by when you can commit to deliver
- Figure out what needs to be done and do it
- Deliver on commitments as promised
- Be reachable and productive from any location

Let's say for a moment you've got this nailed. You hardly ever miss a commitment, thanks to your Getting Things Done system, iCal/GoogleCal/iPhone combo, Franklin planner, or phenomenal memory.

What worked fine when you had three co-located direct reports may buckle when you have ten reports spanning eight time zones. What worked when you traveled two days a month fails when you're on the road two weeks a month. How scalable and portable is your current system?

Navigate the technology-switch trap

You come into a new role, raring to make strategic decisions, wow the market, and inspire your team. Instead, you spend hours trying to make your new Blackberry talk to your company-issued Windows laptop and your home Mac so you can access critical files in the company's proprietary info-management system.

Before your start, find out what communication technologies are used at your new company or your new level. Figure out what programs you'll need for calendar, tasks, and access to crucial company information. For example, does this company use Outlook for calendar/tasks and Salesforce.com for data? Or Google for calendar, your own system for tasks, and SAP for data and processes?

Talk with your go-to tech people. Sometimes they can enter you into systems before your official start date, but often not. What they can usually do is walk you through the options and develop a migration plan.

Also, ask if you can use your best current tools. Some companies have preferences about platforms but don't object to individual choices.

Choose a system that works for you, and work it

Now that you know what the company needs you to use, what else will help you do your work? Will you need to be as efficient at home or on the road as you are in the office? Will others need to access your calendar in real time?

Performance psychologist Jason Womack recommends making time to build your model of a productive day in this new role.[3] In particular, figure out how you will start the day right—typically with a few minutes to determine and document your highest priority for the day. Boost your focus by identifying blocks of time you will need for groups of important tasks. Match these blocks with workspaces—desk, conference room, home, café, outdoors—that minimize interruptions and increase your energy.

Many people still use paper for at least part of their personal set-up. This might be the right time to reconsider. Electronic systems scale in a way that paper and your memory do not.

No tech support? Ask friends who can walk you through the changes, find websites or YouTube videos on how to do whatever tech migration is needed, or pay a personal-hire assistant to help you with this as needed for the first few weeks.

Note that you must actually use your system for it to work. Better to have an imperfect solution you use all the time, than an elegant solution you use half the time.

It might seem odd to draw your attention to something so mundane, but neglecting to adjust task management systems has robbed many new leaders of sleep during their first weeks on the job and torpedoed the trajectories of some. I want better for you.

---

3. Jason Womack, "The Womack Company, Coaching: Maximize Your Time with Individualized Training."
http://www.womackcompany.com/executive-coaching

4 Draft Your Strategic One-Pager

You must have a point of view. From Day One.

As a leader, you can be wrong. You can be misinformed. You can be too pessimistic or optimistic. You cannot be clueless.

Summarize your company's strategy and your team's role

Sit down right now and jot down your thoughts about the industry and company:

- How does your company compete now and with what results?
- How do other companies win in your industry?
- What will drive change in the industry over the next one to five years?
- How are major and emerging competitors, suppliers, and customers addressing these changes?
- What strategy is your company banking on to drive future success, and what is it doing to deliver on that strategy?
- How might your company adjust that strategy to be more successful?

Now take a look at the function or team you'll be leading:

- How does your function and team drive value given the company's current strategy?
- What does the team need to be great at to deliver high value?
- What's your initial take (if only from interviews) on how effective the team is at those capabilities—what are the strengths and gaps?
- What would the team need to be great at if the company were to adjust strategic direction as you described above?

Draft a coherent one-page summary of the state and trends of your industry, company, division/function, and team. Start your job, and become smarter as fast as you can.

If you don't have enough information or insight to take even a stab at answering these questions, you are not ready to start the job. Spend a week learning and thinking.

Do another round of homework and planning

If you are already working at the company, this goes for you, too! When Katie Keating at Adobe moved from marketing leadership to heading a sales organization, she took the time to diagnose—in advance of starting—the state of the group. She then specified what she wanted key people in and around her organization to see and feel at 90 days. Finally, she developed a plan to get there.

Take your query back to your network, focusing as much on products and people as on corporate structure and culture. Stretch your network up, down, and sideways, becoming smarter on company and competitor products, industry practices, and key people in your new world.

Is your predecessor approachable? If so, s/he could be a valuable source of information about the people you'll interact with daily as well as about projects on the horizon.

Hit the Internet again, this time going deep into the search results. Look for news stories, blogs, and academic case studies that can give you glimpses into how your organization's leaders make sense of the market and how they make decisions.

Of course you know not to take everything you hear or read as fact. People will answer your questions from their own perspectives, views that can be colored by experiences good and bad as well as by personal values and philosophies. Expect to hear conflicting reports—there will be a bit of truth in all of them.

Ask for any significant internal documents you can read ahead of time—org chart, business plan, operating manual, budget, whatever is relevant to understanding your group. Search the company on LinkedIn to learn about current employees and roles for which the organization is hiring.

Leaders in nonprofits, education, and government agencies: my recommendations in this Rule apply equally to you. The most productive leaders in your sector think as strategically as their business counterparts. Adjust the wording for your context, and go draft your one-pager.

Whether you have a day or a month before you start, learn what you can, and develop your initial hypotheses about what's going on and your top focus areas. Then, be intensely open to changing your point of view.

5 Take Charge of Your Start

> **"If you plan to show up and do your best, you're still thinking like an individual contributor."**

The courtship is over, and the deal is done. You've accepted the offer, and you've negotiated your start date. Now what?

If you plan to show up and do your best, you're still thinking like an individual contributor. As a leader, you're being watched by a diverse jumble of people in your group and across the organization who are excited and fearful about how their world will change because of the decisions you make.

It's showtime, baby, and you're playing the lead. If you're new to the company or function, you're opening the show with unfamiliar stagehands, an orchestra you've never heard, and a skeptical audience. No one's going to hand you a script, so write your own.

Go beyond any official onboarding

Many companies have an onboarding process—a process for bringing new employees into the organization. You meet with Human Resources about policies and benefits, Facilities about your space, IT about your computer and phone. Some companies even offer executive welcome sessions and peer-led seminars on organizational values and culture. Helpful? Probably. Sufficient? Not even close.

Befriend your brain

Ramping up is hard to do. You'll need to figure out everything from how to address concerns of the major customer who's ready to bolt because his project slipped through the cracks while you were being hired to how to access the company's management reporting system. You could truly make a list of hundreds of things you'll want to figure out in your first month.

Brain science proves that anything unfamiliar takes substantially more brainpower. Driving an unfamiliar route is hugely more costly in brain resources than navigating a familiar route.[4] Using a new cell phone or computer? Expect your productivity to tank until your brain learns to operate the new devices without attention from your tiny, precious pre-frontal cortex.

I want you to appreciate the enormity of what you've taken on—leading a group of people, perhaps in a new company or location, while your brain is distracted by the novelty of everything from your new responsibilities to the ring of your new phone.

So, give yourself every advantage. Do your best to start rested and prepared. If you're making a big leap, you may want to hire a coach who's experienced in helping leaders at your level make a strong start. At least, make a plan.

Write your own onboarding plan

Your plan may include these action items:

- Speak with your entire team to introduce yourself in this role, and make time to speak with them again in probably a couple of weeks when you have more to say
- Meet with each of your direct reports; share with them in advance your basic outline for those conversations
- Meet with your boss and other key leaders with your pocket agenda for each meeting
- Coordinate with your assistant or chief of staff, if you're fortunate enough to have one
- Visit with Security, IT, HR, and Facilities
- Meet your finance rep and HR business partner, if you have them, and figure out how to access your financial and staffing reports
- If you're leading a business unit or sales organization, get on top of the numbers immediately; meet with your CFO or finance contact to check your interpretation
- If you'll be working with cultures unfamiliar to you, arrange a starter tutorial on building business relationships with those cultures
- Reach out to peers you haven't met yet
- Learn the status and history of key initiatives
- Introduce yourself to high-value or strategically important customers and suppliers, and learn their priorities

Develop your plan within your task management system (see Rule #3), so you'll automatically receive reminders, and you'll be able to view and adjust your whole onboarding process as you go.

---

4. David Rock, *Your Brain at Work: Strategies for Overcoming Distraction, Regaining Focus, and Working Smarter All Day Long*, 1 ed. (New York, N.Y.: HarperCollins, 2009).

Part II
Map the Terrain

You've arrived at the meaty part of your start.

The Rules in this section take you from "I'm looking forward to working with you" to "Here's what you can count on our team to deliver."

The most common missteps at this phase include:
- Seeing smoke and running off to chase fires.
- Adopting other people's agendas with insufficient data and thought.
- Becoming buried under the pent-up piles of tasks.
- Either underdoing or overdoing Rule 6—hiding out in your office or schmoozing when you should be planning and committing.

Make your best go at fulfilling these rules within your first two-three weeks. Then learn more and adjust as you go.

- Rule 6: Leverage the Honeymoon
- Rule 7: Map What Matters to People with Power
- Rule 8: Uncover Precisely How Your Group Creates Value
- Rule 9: Figure Out What to Prove by When
- Rule 10: Set Your Milestones

6

Leverage the Honeymoon

"Psychological biases are in your favor—most will want to believe they made a great decision in hiring you."

No matter how thoroughly you looked into the company during the courtship, there will be gaps in your knowledge. Your mission now is to fill in those gaps. Even more important, begin to build communication and trust.

People know you are ramping up. They expect you will have questions. At the same time, they expect you to conduct yourself in a "leaderly" manner, whatever that means to those specific people in your organization's specific culture.

Psychological biases are in your favor—most will want to believe they made a great decision in hiring or promoting you. Those who had no role in hiring you will not be blessed with this bias, yet they will probably want you to succeed so that somebody competent is finally tackling the huge to-do list they've heaped upon your role.

Take advantage of this "grace period" to learn a lot.

Start with your team
Know that when a new leader walks in the door, each team member is asking, "Can I still work here or not?" You may think only the low performers hold this concern; my experience says nearly everyone does. When there's a change of the guard, often the highest performers and brightest-but-miscast players will leave.

Pay primary attention to your team for the first month or two. They need to experience how much you value them—in their roles and as individuals. You communicate this value not by praise—it's too early for that to mean much—but by asking thoughtful questions and listening intently.

Some new leaders invite their team members to jot a get-to-know-me email about their personal and professional backgrounds and goals. Others schedule 1:1 time with each. (See Rule #16 for topics to cover.)

Connect up, across, and out

As a senior partner in a global accounting firm told me, "Managing across and down are important, but if you don't manage up you're toast."

Up is not just your boss. Up includes each member of the executive team or boss' peers who control access to resources you need. For C-levels and nonprofit executive directors, communicate 1:1 with your board members and major investors or donors early.

After engaging your team and executives, go out to the field—do a "ride-along" with sales, visit some branches, stores, or plants. If you don't have a travel budget, use desktop videoconferencing so you can see each other's faces.

Introduce yourself to key people outside your organization with a ten- to fifteen-minute call or thirty-minute coffee. Customers and suppliers won't expect you to know everything yet, and they'll usually be glad to give you an earful about what you should be doing.

People will make time for you...use it well

Many leaders appreciate talking with someone new to the company or department. Some call it "reverse onboarding"—they want to hear your fresh insights about the company and industry.

Come curious and committed, with good questions. Prepare, but don't tightly control the conversation. As one of my experienced CEO interviewees said, "You have just a couple months to craft these bonds. The conversations are worth it, even if just idle discovery."

Review your strategic one-pager (see Rule #4) before meetings, and come ready to test your point of view. Share your thinking, if appropriate, framed as "I've been wondering how X is affecting Y." Ask, "What are your thoughts?" Listen for the pace at which decisions are made and tasks are implemented, so you can create reasonable date targets for your first initiatives.

Expect to be asked about you...your background, your experiences, why you're here in this role. Be professional—never bash a former employer or divulge confidential information—and be real.

7

Map What Matters to People with Power

If you're going to deliver for someone, make it your priority to deliver up. That gives you breathing room to deliver for everyone else.

Figure out who holds power

You know where to start: your boss, plus your boss's boss and/or board of directors.

To determine the rest of your list, ask

- Who above you in the organization will freak if you fail to deliver on commitments? This probably includes some of your boss' peers.
- Who, if they slacked off for a month, could destroy your ability to deliver? This includes most, perhaps all, of your directs.
- Who else must continue to cooperate for you to meet your significant commitments? Consider key customers, firms running important and hard-to-replace outsourced operations, and suppliers of critical components.

I call these people "powerholders"—the subset of your stakeholders who can make a real difference in your ability to deliver and reap rewards.

Map what you want from each other

Create a "Power Map." Make a spreadsheet, with a row for each powerholder or group of similar powerholders. Add these columns to your spreadsheet and drop in some bullet points. Or, if you're comfortable with mind-mapping or organization chart software, make an org chart and annotate it with this information:

- On what bases are they formally rewarded: Sales? Variance from budget? Share price? How often: Quarterly? Annually? On what sets of data: Accounting data? CRM monthly reports? An industry report?
- What informal rewards are important to them: Industry visibility? Support for their "brand"—running a tight ship, being a great mentor, pulling off the impossible?
- What do they want from you/your role: No surprises? Achieving the quarterly sales target? New products to market faster than their peers' divisions?
- What do you want from them?

Catalog what you can do for (and to) each other

How could they help you get what you want? How could you help them get what they want?

Make sure to consider this question both from the capabilities you have today and from possibilities for the future. For example, your head of R&D wants external visibility as a leader in green materials. Later this year you'll be starting work on next generation, eco-savvy products. You could offer her the opportunity to become the public face of this initiative. In *Influence Without Authority*, Cohen and Bradford catalog ways you can build your power by helping others get what they want.[5] Make a habit of noting what's important to the people you meet and identifying early and appropriate opportunities to use your resources to be of service.

If you're in a tough environment, you'd be wise also to keep an eye for the rough stuff. What could they do to you (especially below the radar) if they want to turn up the pressure on your group? Refrain from labeling people as "friendly" or "unfriendly" to you and your team; instead identify the current and potential flows of information, money, and support between your group and theirs.

Now, identify other stakeholders and their interests

When you can take a few more minutes, add the other groups of people who are interested in what you do and could help or hinder, but don't meet the power criteria above. Often these include

- People who were passed over for your job
- Junior players who want to hitch to your star
- Diversity groups across the firm
- Customers (if your own customers are internal)
- Consultants who have worked with your group
- Who else is relevant for you?

Update your map as power shifts

Calendar a meeting with yourself at least quarterly to update your map. Consider the relationships between your powerholders and other stakeholders—who listens to whom. Determine your next actions to delight, satisfy, or minimize damage for your powerholders.

---

5. Allen R. Cohen and David L. Bradford, *Influence Without Authority*, 2nd ed. (Hoboken, NJ: John Wiley & Sons, 2005).

8 Uncover Precisely How Your Group Creates Value

"Identify together the couple things your group does that generate the most value to the organization."

Let's say you're head of an internal consulting group at a technology company. Your mission is clear: your team creates value by adapting your firm's software to meet specific needs of major customers, which contributes to revenue by attracting and retaining these customers.

Or, maybe that's just part of the story. Maybe your group drives additional value...even most of its value...as a training ground for future leaders of the systems consulting division. Maybe your group functions as the eyes and ears of product marketing, driving crucial innovation. Or, maybe your unit exists because of a horse-trade to balance power among the heads of Marketing, Sales, and Engineering.

You gotta know. Said Bruce McNamer, CEO of TechnoServe, "God help you putting your stamp on an organization if you have little knowledge of it."

What does your group really do? And who cares?

How do your team members describe the work product of the group? Their customers? Their suppliers? Their competition? What do they think about each day?

Make your own observations. Watch how your team members spend their time. Take a look at what they actually give internal or external customers as their work product.

Who cares what your group does? Make a list. Start with customers or groups downstream (groups that do something with your team's output). What do they receive from your group? What do they do with it? What parts of your output do they really use? What parts do they discard or under-use? How do they modify your output to make it more valuable?

Now consider upstream groups. What do they gain from your team? Surprisingly generous internal pricing credit? Customer knowledge? Technical know-how? Look, too, at adjacent groups that make use of your people or knowledge.

Within three to six months, you can refine your idea of who values what by looking for discrepancies between the reactions you expect and the reactions you see as you deliver. Who's unexpectedly impressed or thankful? Who is puzzlingly silent?

What else does your group do that drives value?

Gather a few perceptive team members and together sketch a quick map of how product, people, knowledge, and money flow through your group over time. Identify together the things your group does that generate the most value to the organization. You might create a "value stream map" outlining for each product or service the paths to delivering value to customers.

Look for bottlenecks, including ways your group might be a bottleneck. What gets stuck in your people's inboxes? What does your group hoard? What are they chronically short of? How does your group put the brand at risk?

How is this picture changing?

Which of these factors are becoming substantially more or less important? What's driving those trends? Look for discontinuous change, too. For example, once the new web self-service capability is upgraded in a couple months, what's the impact on your customer support engineering team?

If your organization has similar groups in other geographies or business units, talk with the leaders of those groups and compare notes on what you do that drives value and how this is changing.

What's in your control?

As you investigate these questions, you'll learn a lot about what your group decides and what they take as given. Start to inventory the decisions about products, people, and processes that are

- yours to make on your own
- yours to make subject to approval
- yours to propose
- within your opportunity to influence

When I say "yours," for this first pass I mean anyone in your group. Over time, you'll become clear who really has control and influence regarding which decisions.

9 Figure Out What to Prove by When

"There's always something to prove, and faster than you'd like."

"Internal promotes have to show the goods faster."

"External hires are more under the gun for quick wins."

"Acquisition hires have the hardest start."

"You have 6 months." "You have 90 days." "You have 30 days."

On no topic was there less agreement among the executives I interviewed. My take: it's all hard. There's always something to prove, and faster than you'd like.

To keep focused rather than frantic, start with two categories and three time horizons:

- Categories: What does my team need to deliver? What do I need to prove about me?
- Time horizons: immediate (typically one to two months), near-term (two to five months), first year (six to twelve months).

Determine whether smoke means fire

Sometimes you'll be forced into playing firefighter immediately. If that's the case, rush to the scene of the inferno, grab a hose, do your best to find qualified firefighters, and get back to your real job of leading your group to results.

Says Bart Fisher, Organizational Development strategist for technology companies: "Figure out if you need a firefighter or a weatherman. Is it smoke because there's a problem, or fog because there's uncertainly? If smoke, fight the fire. If fog, take the time you need to figure out what's going on."

If there's no fire, hold off on major decisions for at least a month, so you can assess the situation.

Figure out what your team has to prove by when

Your organization is scrutinizing your team as follows:

*   Results—are you delivering the goods as promised?
*   Competence—are you a capable group or a bunch of amateurs who got lucky and hit the targets? Figure out what signifies competency. (Hint: this may have little to do with actual functional proficiency.)
*   Workload and hustle—are you working your tails off—short of burning people out? (Hint: others may confuse hustle with value, you do not.)
*   Compliance—are you achieving your miracles legitimately or through shortcuts and shenanigans that put the company at risk?

Inventory who's watching your team for what factors, and what they expect to see by when. Doing this will also help you identify opportunities to educate your powerholders about metrics more useful than the ones they're tracking now.

Figure out what you have to prove about YOU

The obvious answer is, you have to prove to your higher-ups that you are capable of running your group so you hit the targets, preferably with minimal organizational or customer chaos. Beyond that, you'd like to prove that whatever major weaknesses they thought you had when they hired you either are not so bad or that you've taken wise steps to minimize the impact.

Identify your short set of priorities

Phyllis Stewart Pires, Cisco veteran and now Director of Community Experience at SAP, set a thirty-day goal to provide a summary back to the organization of her key findings "based on my early listening and learning, and a draft of what actions I intend to take based on those learnings. I invite them to let me know if I'm on target or missing any major issues. I'm often told that this demonstration of actually listening and then 'getting it' creates an early trust that helps make changes to the organization that might otherwise have been resisted."

It's up to you to take all this input and figure out what's most important. In addition to more detailed notes for yourself, draft a short set of bullets on what you aim for your team to accomplish by when. Work these through with key members of your team, your advisors, and your leadership.

Address how you'll handle targets committed by your predecessor. Often, especially in large companies and in fairly stable units, you'll be expected at least to meet the previous targets in addition to any further priorities you identify. Take these pass-through targets into account before committing your team to other accomplishments.

Set Your Milestones

Tony Levitan, founder of Egreetings and other ventures, said, "I've seen lots of great ways to start. Some people sit back and watch. Others wade in and stand shoulder to shoulder."

There are, of course, hazards to either approach. Some new hires waste their goodwill period pondering and find themselves irrelevant. Others wade in so quickly and so deeply that midway across the stream they realize they're in far over their heads—in the wrong stream. Your wise plan will balance diagnosis and action.

Set realistic milestones for the big stuff

What are the one to three big outputs the organization is counting on your team to deliver, and what needs to happen fast to ensure success?

Start your plan with those "big rocks," filling in the "pebbles" of smaller projects as you can. Meanwhile, let the "sand" of non-important organizational silt pass through your filter unheeded.

Be realistic about how fast you can drive change. Most people do not like change. Organizations are made of people. Organizations do not like change. Organizations generate "immune systems" to knock change out of the system.

Yes, when you were being wooed to this job, you heard, "We're expecting big things from you. You're just the person we need to accelerate acquisitions, raise the effectiveness of the sales force, transform back-end processes, make R&D more strategy-driven..." Chances are, what they meant was, "No one here is willing to roll that big boulder uphill. We are glad you're game to try."

Don't shy away from the "big rocks," but do be realistic. When you're setting milestones, give yourself enough time to uncover the immune system response, weaken it proactively by building powerful support, and diffuse it by managing the change process well. Typically this takes more time and energy than making the change itself.

Guide your team in writing the roadmap

Your team can't function without the basics...Where are we going?, How will we get there?, Who will need to do what?

If you are the only person in your group with a functioning neocortex, feel free to write the plan all by yourself. (You might also look for a new group.) Otherwise, creating the roadmap is best done with intense collaboration across your team. If they're inexperienced in planning, and you need to plan quickly, interview them, develop a draft roadmap, then improve it with team input.

Use Discovery-Driven planning

Twenty years of watching strategic plans trashed by reality has made me a big fan of Discovery-Driven planning.[6]

Make a flexible roadmap. Highlight the uncertainties, document your assumptions, and plan for contingencies. Plan ways to gather the info needed for each decision point, make decisions at that point, and figure out how that adjustment needs to ripple through the process your team and others are executing.

Prepare to disappoint some people

Of course, people don't like to hear "no." At times, though, it's the only possible answer. No, because we cannot tackle another project this week (or this month) and do our best work. No, because that project isn't a good fit with the team's current goals or mission.

When possible, match that "no" with a time frame or a conversation about options. No, we can't do it this month with our existing work load, but is there something else of lesser priority that we could defer so we can tackle the new project now? No, because this project doesn't fit with existing processes, but it sounds like a great idea. Maybe we should consider shifting the process. Let's arrange time next quarter to put our heads together about that.

---

6. Rita Gunther McGrath and Ian C MacMillan, "Discovery-Driven Planning," *Harvard Business Review*, July 1, 1995.

Part III
Show Up Wisely

Musicians have instruments, surgeons have tools, engineers have software, and leaders have...themselves. That's it.

Know what you've got to offer, and bring out what's needed now.

- Rule 11: Apply Your Strengths—and Beware
- Rule 12: Deal with Your Weak Spots
- Rule 13: (Re)Introduce Yourself Internally and Externally
- Rule 14: Don't Blame the Last Guy
- Rule 15: Show People How to Work with You
- Rule 16: Get Over Yourself

11 Apply Your Strengths— and Beware

"In our research, 'lack of weaknesses' was not the distinguishing feature of the best leaders. Instead, they possessed a few profound strengths."
- Zenger, et al

We know from decades of research that "fatal flaws" can derail your leadership path.[7] What we also know is the power of impressive strengths to drive leadership success, regardless of soft spots in the rest of your profile.

Use your strengths to do the heavy lifting of making a strong start.

Be specific—what are you really good at?

Sometimes executive clients point to successes as evidence of their strengths. Just because you've achieved a great outcome doesn't mean you aced all the inputs. For example, the outstanding ROI of your ad campaign doesn't mean the creative you designed was all that great. Maybe you had so-so creative and really smart media buys.

Instead of equating your successes with your strengths, use your record of successes (and "failures") as a starting place for identifying what you tend to do—do you usually identify the problem? Contribute new ideas? Structure the decision options? Analyze the data?

Then, consider—of the things you typically do, which are actually strengths. Just because you typically do something doesn't actually mean you're great at it! Even top executives are well-practiced at many things they do rather badly. For example, most leaders run meetings, and most meetings are run poorly.

---

7. Michael M. Lombardo and Robert W. Eichinger, *Preventing Derailment: What to Do Before It's Too Late, 1st ed. Technical Report Series* (138g, Greensboro, NC: CCL Press, 1989).

So, how do you know what you actually do well?

- Ask people who know you well. It's not too hard to find people who will tell the truth about your strengths. Ask your former colleagues to email you back with three to five specific things you do very well, compared to others at your level and function.
- Look for evidence. Are you asked to present to high-stakes clients more frequently than your peers are? Hypothesis worth checking: you're great at client presentations. Or maybe, you do above-average presentations, but you shine at performing under pressure. Check your previous reviews and 360s for evidence of strengths. (High-performers often only remember the few weaknesses noted, so go back and read the actual reviews.)
- Use strength-focused assessments and interpret them thoughtfully. See Appendix D for my top resources for understanding your strengths, including the Myers-Briggs Type Indicator® and the Strengths-Finder®.

Beware diagnosing problems to suit your strengths

Carl Spetzler, CEO of Strategic Decisions Group, talks about our tendency to "drag the problem into our own comfort zone."[8] If you're good at running numbers, be aware that you may frame problems quantitatively, when lack of strategic insight is at the root of the problem. If you're great at persuasion, you may mistake an analytical problem for a communication opportunity.

Seeing problems as they really are—rather than as you are—is especially essential in your first months on the job. Chances are your team and peers will give you some rope to "tackle problems in your own way." Unless you check that impulse to show how good you are by mis-applying your strengths, that could be enough rope to hang you.

Figure out which strengths matter now

Strengths overused or applied at the wrong time are no help at all. Expect your new position to require you to draw on different strengths from your last.

A client respected for driving processes and making well-considered decisions was promoted to lead a group ten times bigger. Suddenly her day was filled with unanticipated people problems. She kept reaching for processes, only to discover they weren't really there, and she didn't have enough knowledge of this function to create processes quickly. So, she had to draw on long-undervalued strengths in making decisions fast and inspiring junior leaders.

Your new role may make good use of strengths you forgot you had. Let it! Put on ice your strengths that aren't needed now, and use what's relevant.

---

8. Carl Spetzler. "Neuroscience and the Four Functions in Decision-Making." Presentation to Bay Area Association for Psychological Type. February 13, 2010.

Deal with Your Weak Spots

"For your first few months in a new job, you'll achieve more by leveraging your strengths."

What does Miriam Rivera, former VP Legal at Google turned early-stage investor, look for in leaders?[9] People wise enough to admit their weaknesses.

When you remember your weaknesses, you're more likely to arrange the conditions—budget, technology, people—under which you and your team can be successful.

Also, when you make peace with your weaknesses and foibles, that takes away their power to flummox you. You don't have to look ridiculous trying to pretend you're perfect.

You're about to make some big commitments to results on behalf of you and your team. Before you do, wouldn't it make sense to remind yourself what you do very badly? And have a plan for what to do should those skills become important? You have three ways to deal with your weaknesses—improve, punt, or pay.

Improve

Skip this. What?? How could I—as a coach who has seen how thoroughly people can develop—suggest you don't improve on your weaknesses?

---

9. Pam Fox Rollin "Weekly Leader Podcast Episode 41 - Miriam Rivera, Ulu Ventures," March 8, 2010, http://weeklyleader.net/2010/weekly-leader-podcast -episode-41-miriam-rivera-ulu-ventures/

Right now you don't have time. Turning weak areas into areas of decent performance usually takes substantial focus over a period of months. For your first few months, you'll achieve more by leveraging your strengths.

Exception: if your weak areas include listening to others, deciding on priorities, or organizing yourself to meet commitments—you will have to address these right from the start.

Punt

I worked with a fast-growing new media company where both founders share the same personality type. Together, they've painted the big picture opportunity, rallied funders and hires, thumbnailed the strategy, hopped on planes to engage customers, and mentored their team through example and debate. They're moving fast, so they've focused on what comes most easily, given their personality types.[10]

At the same time, they're smart enough to know the company needs tasks accomplished that are, for them, a drain on their energy. So, they've taken care to hire people who enjoy logistics, stay steady through change, and will actually make time to enter the customer data in the darn database.

As these guys know, for every weakness you have, there are people for whom this is a strength. Just make sure you put them on your team, instead of surrounding yourself with people just like you. Then, give them room and respect so they can do their magic while you do yours.

Pay

Expertise is everywhere. But it does not want to be free.

Need to create a financial model? Design a compelling slide presentation? Make your website more relevant to global markets? There are fine people who spend all day doing this and only this. Often you can contract for brief, specific engagements. Your network can help you find these experts efficiently.

If you work for a company that budgets as if you should already know how to do everything, or has an onerous vendor qualification process, you'll need to be creative. If the skills are in your company, see if you can arrange an informal trade of time. Or, see if you can punt the project to another group until you can bring those skills into your group.

While you're ramping up, take on work that relies on your weak areas only if

- it's OK to do it badly,
- it can be punted to someone else, or
- you can pay an expert to do it for you.

---

10. Both are ENTP on the Myers-Briggs Type Indicator®. For more on personality type, see Appendix D.

13

(Re)Introduce Yourself Internally & Externally

"Are you the next trainee manager on rotation, or the superstar poached from the competition?"

The new division head wasn't welcome. As an egghead policy wonk hired to lead a long-term group of mostly ex-military tough guys, he knew it was going to be tough to earn their respect. He also knew if he could talk with them as people, they'd cut him more slack than if they spent the first month talking about him as a figurehead, the corner-office jerk whose name now appeared at the bottom of memos.

So, right away he called everyone together. He acknowledged that it would take time for him to know them. He told his story of how he grew up, what led him to make the choices he did, and what it meant to him to be here. The stories he chose demonstrated that he shared their values, if not their career path. Brief, memorable, and meaningful, this meeting bought him the time he needed to prove his worth to the group.

Find out who they think you are

Before your new colleagues learn anything about you as a person, they have an impression of who you're supposed to be. Are you the bozo from HQ sent to "clean up" this renegade plant? Are you the whiz kid who's expected to save the division? Are you the next trainee manager on rotation, or the superstar poached from the competition?

When you pitch your story—any story—know that it will be heard through a filter of history and expectations.

Craft your messages

Your introduction will include only a portion of your professional and personal history, so you might as well pick the values and priorities that are likely to guide your leadership, at this time, in this role.

As you speak to your team, is it time for a story of persistence in the face of odds? Of cooperation and sacrifice for the common good? Of truth-telling, care-giving, or house-cleaning?

As you speak across the organization, identify which themes are most critical. Are you offering a fresh perspective from an analogous industry (with appropriate humility about your need to learn this one) or proven techniques from another division? Will it serve you to be understood as the change agent on a mission, or an enthusiastic soldier for the strategy?

As you speak to customers, suppliers, and the marketplace, what messages are most critical? Which must you avoid?

Craft a coherent story about You

Today more than ever, these stories need to form a coherent whole. If you're a public figure—and with LinkedIn, you probably are—your employees, customers, suppliers, and executive team have access to the same information about you. Figure your employees will be reading your customers' blogs, and vice-versa. No longer can you design different personas for different audiences. However, you can and should be thoughtful about which areas to emphasize to each audience. If you have access to a good corporate communications team, involve them early in crafting the broader message.

Says Amari Romero Thomas, SVP of United Way, Silicon Valley, "The higher up you go, the more transparent you need to be about who you are and what you are doing."

Switch to a story about We

Once most people know who you are and what you're about, it's time to stop talking about you. (Save your favorite stories about you for when you're invited to speak at your high school's commencement.) Now it's time to talk about your team—what they're committed to accomplishing, how they're serving the organization, and what they need from the rest of the organization. (See Rule #16.)

14 Don't Blame the Last Guy

"He knew what you don't, yet."

You would never stoop to blame. Or would you?

You're going to be tempted

Especially if the person who last had the job was let go, demoted, or otherwise removed, you'll be tempted. But even if the last guy was elevated to his/her next walk-on-water job, you're still going to be tempted to blame him for your team's problems.

After all, if the last guy was so great, he wouldn't have left the department in the mess you now find. He would have picked all those "low-hanging fruit" you see dangling all over the department. He would have fired the performance problems and supported the stars. He would have generated the monthly metrics that are so obviously needed, and he would have tied up the loose ends now filling your inbox.

He knew what you don't, yet

He knew that it made no sense to run reports based on the crappy data coming in from the field. He knew that the "performance problem" had a personal dispute with your boss, who threw him under the bus at rating time. He knew that picking the "low-hanging fruit" wouldn't turn the department around, so he focused on what was more important.

You will look foolish, and your team will let you

Your team members will happily collude in your assessment that the last guy was incompetent. Gets the focus off them. Gives them hope that you'll be better.

Until you start making the same mistakes. Or, more likely, different ones. Chances are good that you will notice opportunities he didn't. You will make some hard calls that he shied away from. You will create smart new metrics he never considered. And, some of these new initiatives will blow up in your face, just as he did. And then your blame game is going to look very, very foolish.

Even if this guy was a real screw-up, skip the blame. As one of my interviewees said, "Why should I blame my predecessor? My team will do that for me."

View the last guy as your teacher

Go learn what you can about the trade-offs he saw, the battles he was fighting, the opportunities he never took time to pursue. If you can find him, ask him what he would do if he had another year or two in the job. Ask him about the hardest parts of the job...he'll probably be glad to tell you, maybe over a beer.

If you don't have access to him, apply your forensic anthropology skills. What do his metrics suggest was important to him? What initiatives did he sponsor? What were his "failures," and what can you learn about the root causes?

Be gracious. If this guy is still at your company—or hanging out with your team, or writing an industry blog—what he thinks matters, at least a little. You are standing on the shoulders (or graves) of many. It's worth your time to learn their legacy. By acting with maturity, appreciating whatever he did accomplish for your group, and continuing to seek his counsel if appropriate, you benefit from his stumbles. At least then you can make *new* mistakes.

That said, be realistic about what you've inherited

You may have noticed that public company CEOs surface bad news in the first quarter of their tenure. Find the problems in your group fast, so you can tackle them before you are seen to own their creation.

Put together a brief presentation or talking points for your leadership team about the state of your group as you find it. Describe without blame how the group is doing relative to history, targets, and market opportunity. Offer your work-in-progress viewpoint on what's contributing positively and negatively to performance and what changes you plan to make.

15

Show People How to Work with You

"Often new leaders neglect to tell their people what they want...and then are frustrated when they don't get it."

You've got your own way of doing things. You'll adapt them to the new culture and business situation. Still, you'll probably want to keep doing some things in ways that have worked for you before.

Don't make 'em guess

So says Steven Aldrich, CEO of PositScience and former business leader at Intuit. He laid out for me the conversations he has with directs when he starts a new role. "Here's how I've done it in the past. Explain to me how you do it here. Let's see which of these ways, or some other better way, will work for us now."

Often new leaders neglect to tell their people what they want...and then are frustrated when they don't get it. When your direct reports have ideas, do you want to see first a thoughtful proposal with data or a text message asking you for a time to think it through together. A couple of my executive clients are intensely annoyed by people who check email during meetings. Others want their reports to check email during long meetings. Tell your people which camp you're in.

When you make them guess, they're likely to guess wrong. Then, you're likely to be annoyed and start to doubt their competence, forgetting that your frustration rests with you and how you like to work.

Make it easy to work with you

Here's what to tell them:
- What to include in a weekly status update and when to send it
- How you define urgent information or questions
- How to reach you with urgent information or questions

- What response time you expect from your emails or voicemails to them, and under what conditions (if any) you expect them to check emails, text, or voicemails during off-hours
- What short list of behaviors are absolutely essential for members of your team and managers/leaders in your organization
- Any of your triggers that they need to know to stay on your good side

Of course, you want to know all this about your new boss, too! Best source: the executive assistant, if there is one.

Tie it back to purpose

When you can tie your preferences to shared business goals and values, you'll seem less petty and idiosyncratic.

For Steven Aldrich, politicking is a major peeve. Why? Covert agendas and behind-back actions destroy the trust and open vetting of ideas critical to team effectiveness.

For Amari Romero-Thomas, SVP—United Way, Silicon Valley, face-to-face communication is vital. Going to see the person you want to influence or support demonstrates respect, and two-way conversation gets to the heart of the matter faster than any email chain.

Show, invite, tell, problem-solve, reinforce

- Show people what you're doing: put your own cell away at the beginning of your team meeting.
- Invite people to join in your preference: "I'll be keeping my focus here when I'm with you. I've asked my assistant to step in if there's an emergency while we're together. You are welcome to ask him to do the same for you."
- Tell: "I prefer cell phones quiet and away when we meet."
- Problem-solve: "Anyone anticipate they may be called away during our meeting? You're welcome to let your team know to contact my assistant if there's an urgent interruption."
- Reinforce: "I appreciated your full attention during our conversation. For me, that makes our meeting more efficient."

Be reasonable

A side benefit of cataloging your preferences: you're likely to behave more intentionally. If you say you expect people to note their to-dos during meetings, you will do it, too.

Pick your battles, and make them good ones. If you can't find a business purpose for your little bugaboo, let it go. Insisting your directs provide a purpose when they block time on your calendar is reasonable. Insisting they never use exclamation marks in internal memos is not!

16 Get Over Yourself

> **"Your team members will give you the goods only to the degree they trust you to act in their best interests."**

Here's an annoying irony: the longer you've done the job search or promotion process, the more rough your start.

If you've been job hunting, you've spent a lot of time talking about your strengths and accomplishments. Or, if you were just promoted, you may have been kicking it hard to make it to the top of the candidate list. You've been focused on making your numbers, communicating your accomplishments, and sprucing yourself up to look like you're ready for the next level.

In short, you've been focusing on YOU. However, focusing on yourself is a quick road to failure as a leader. Now's the time to turn it around and focus on your team.

Find out who they are and what they want

I was coaching a CEO through his first round of feedback, which included team frustration with their lack of connection with him and the shortage of professional opportunities and guidance he provided. I asked him about the conversations he had with team members about what's important to them personally and to their professional goals. "Uh oh, I never asked them that," he said. "When I started, I asked them what their job was, why it's important, and what they needed from me. Wow, I guess I should find out more about them." Yep.

Here's what you want to learn, over time, about each team member

- What are you working on?
- What do you enjoy the most and the least about your job?
- What is going well on this team? What's going less well?

- How could this group be even more successful?
- What do you do well? What do you want to do more of?
- What do you do less well? What do you want to do less of?
- What helps you be most productive?
- Where do you want to be professionally in five to ten years? One to two years?
- What do you think you need to do to get there?

Through these conversations, you want to learn how team members think about themselves, what they're committed to accomplish, how they handle commitments and tradeoffs, what they're worried about, how resilient they're feeling, who they're close with and who they find difficult, and what they want from you.

Build trust with your team members

Earning and keeping the trust of your team is one of your most important challenges as a leader. Why would they entrust you, some stranger or the idiot who was promoted ahead of them, with this valuable information? Your team members will give you the goods only to the degree they trust you to act in their best interests.

Make it easier for them to do their jobs. If they need access to financial data, talk with the controller's office and make it happen. If they need a better relationship with Marketing, coach them through it. If they really need better computers, arrange new computers if you can. Yes, there's a limit to the goodies you can dole out. You're not the candy man, and they may be able to do more with less. Focus on clearing the biggest obstacles, then hold them accountable for results.

Speak well of your team around the company and beyond

I've seen leaders at all levels shoot themselves in the foot by talking down their team. Don't do it! Dissing your team won't make you look street smart and won't protect you from responsibility for their performance. Instead, it will diminish your team's influence across the organization, making their performance worse. Plus, you will look petty and ineffective.

When you do need to speak with other leaders or even customers about your team's challenges, do it in a mature way.

More often, look for appropriate ways to showcase the skills, wise action, and accomplishments of specific team members and your team as a whole.

Part IV
Start Your Wins

Now, you're starting to deliver.

Chances are you're in this job because you're good at "the work." You know what you're doing as a marketer, systems architect, biochemist, or whatever brought you to this point.

So these Rules focus on the "soft skills" that make a real difference.

Teams live and die by the quality of their communication. What sort of conversations will happen more often because you are here? Who will be included, and which voices will be heard? What fresh understandings will be created because of how you speak and listen?

This is the most powerful time for you to upgrade the conversations on your team. Seize the opportunity!

- Rule 17: Pick Smart Quick Wins
- Rule 18: Plant Seeds for Future Wins
- Rule 19: Tune Up Your Team
- Rule 20: Communicate Early and Often
- Rule 21: Tell a Good Story
- Rule 22: Bring Value to Any Room
- Rule 23: Balance Curiosity, Advice, and Silence

Pick Smart Quick Wins

"Choose your target well."

You want to prove you're the hotshot they're hoping they hired. So, you're going to kick your group into high gear and start racking up wins.

Not so fast, grasshopper. Bruce McNamer of TechnoServe: "As a first-time CEO, I put pressure on myself to do something dramatic. I wish I had given myself a little more time to learn." Monique Connor, highly-respected PricewaterhouseCoopers partner, put it this way: "Quick wins? Does your organization actually need quick wins?"

How could anything be wrong with a quick win? Well, new leaders often lack perspective and pick the wrong target, they gun for wins instead of helping the department transition to new leadership, and they often damage people and process.

Pick your target carefully

I know, you're still absolutely convinced you need at least one quick win. Fine. Choose your target well.

When Steven Aldrich became CEO of Posit Science, he saw right away from customer and employee feedback that the supply chain was broken. He considered having an external group come in and fix it. He then considered having a supply chain consultant instead coach his team on how to do it. That would take just a little longer, but it would leave the team more capable of solving problems in the future and able to take full credit for the win. Smart choice.

Look for a project that hits as many of these criteria as possible:
- Makes a real impact on the P&L
- Seen as a win by people with power (See Rule #7)
- Relieves a significant pain for your team

- Can be replicated, rolled out, or scaled up
- Engages a cross-section of people on your team
- Generates learning that makes your team more capable of future wins

From a recent promote to VP Engineering at a global software company: "Because I was promoted from within, I knew which issues were causing pain. With my team, I prioritized the top five problems, and I solved two of them right away. That meant dealing with some unpleasant organizational politics, which was risky. Taking that risk earned a lot of respect from the team."

Make the process a win

"My most disastrous hires," said Rob Hurlbut, CEO of Attune Foods and former CEO of Niman Ranch, "thought they had a clear mandate. Instead of building buy-in, they chose to drive it themselves."

How you achieve that win is at least as important as which win you select.[11] Are you going to seize on your first idea, cram it down their throats, ride herd, and take credit? Of course not. (Though many do.)

You are going to identify the project collectively with many on your team, invite participation, coach or even work shoulder to shoulder, and give the team the win. You are going to go for the win in a way that leaves your team more capable of delivering future wins.

Include your skeptics, as long as they're willing to do the work. Give them time to become believers. Invite, rather than coerce.

Stay focused on what matters

The quick wins you choose will signal to others what matters to you. A CMO I coached chose to implement a long-discussed marketing dashboard as her first win. Her team got the message: this ship now runs on data.

Finally, it's no win to let the core business stumble while you chase fast glory. Figure out what portion of your time must be spent to keep the widgets rolling, and keep your priorities straight.

---

11. Mark E. Van Buren and Todd Safferstone, "The Quick Wins Paradox," *Harvard Business Review*, January 2009, 54–61.

18 Plant Seeds for Future Wins

"Bold moves in the second and third quarters of your tenure tend to accelerate your career."

Some leaders chase quick wins, one after the other. That can work for a while, especially in rapidly-changing industries. Still, most leadership roles worth having require wise decisions to build the next years of business success.

Start seeding medium-term wins

Even if your organization's planning process doesn't require you to create a high-level project plan for each strategic objective, do it anyway. That way you'll have thought through how to accomplish each objective, and you'll know how much lead time your group will need.

Planning for wins in a methodical way will enable you to figure out what resources you need to acquire or build early. If your legal department is weak, you can probably pay for outside contracting expertise when you need it. However, if your biz dev team is unused to approaching bigger companies, you'll probably need to start working on this soon. Give yourself enough run time this year to create next year's wins.

Be bold!

If you want a mediocre career, play it safe at every turn. If you want to gain the resources to accomplish more and more, you must take risks.

Here's a pattern I've noticed among my clients at all levels: bold moves in the second and third quarters of your tenure tend to accelerate your career. Your first quarter, you usually don't know enough and don't have enough support to pick the right bold moves. By your fourth quarter, you'd have to overcome perception as a ho-hum performer.

As a fairly new Senior Manager at Accenture, I challenged the thinking of a C-level executive at a Fortune 50 client and within an afternoon turned that conversation into a half-million dollar project for my team, repositioning the client in key marketplaces within six months. Could I have annoyed him instead? Yes. Would I have been fired for that? Possibly, but probably not, with the credibility I'd built. Worth the risk? Absolutely. The trajectory of the timid lies far below the path of the prudently bold.

Don't let others make decisions for you

Ann Klein, formerly a senior executive at Siebel Systems and now a consultant, described times when she was under pressure early in her tenure to make specific decisions and take on other executives' causes. It took a lot of backbone and humility to say, "I don't know enough about the problem yet to come to that, or any, solution."

You will likely face pressure to apply others' judgments before developing your own. Find the fortitude to reach your own conclusions. Like Ann, most of the executives I've known who found that courage were glad they did.

Find the leverage point for change

If you've ever consulted, I bet you've noticed that the problem you're hired to solve often is not the real problem. Usually, parts of a system have gotten out of alignment, wobbling more and more over time. When the performance impact of that wobble hits the numbers, suddenly "something must be done...fast!" So, a problem-focused task force is assembled and whacks at whatever part of the problem is visible from their conference room.

The leverage point for effective change is often just out of scope of the problem. Start looking systematically for opportunities to improve processes or make powerful changes.

Keep building relationships as you generate wins

You don't know at this stage who is going to be key to your success. Maybe it's the administrative assistant who has tight rein on your CEO's calendar, or maybe it's the financial guru who knows where to find pockets of discretionary spending. At a minimum, be considerate and efficient when asking for their help. Better, keep learning what would interest them about initiatives you have in mind.

"The higher you go in an organization, the more people that want you to fail," I heard a senior technology executive say. Best antidote: becoming known over months and years as a powerful ally as well as a high performer.

19 Tune Up Your Team

"Once direction is set, your fundamental job as a leader is a hunter, curator, and builder of talent."

You know you're going to be accountable for results. So, you are accountable for staffing and organizing your team to deliver those results.

Many leaders, especially less experienced ones, are reluctant to take responsibility for that second piece. Even if you've inherited a team widely recognized as superb, goals may be served by bringing on people with new capabilities, swapping or redefining roles, and releasing people whose skills and ambitions fit better elsewhere.

Once direction is set, your fundamental job as a leader is hunter, curator, and builder of talent.

See who you have

- Do I have the right people—skills, capabilities, attitude?
- Are they in the right roles?
- Are they focused on the right things?
- Which improvements are coachable in a relevant time frame and which are not?

Don't overreact to their reactions to you

Your team members are dealing with their own issues about having a new boss. Some will grumble to your face. Some will schmooze you. Others will hide. (Yes, these are grown-ups we're talking about.)

Do not mistake these reactions to the situation for competence at their jobs or even openness to embracing your new way of doing things. The grumbler may become your strongest ally.

Research shows that your smartest team members are among the most likely to challenge your decisions, push your buttons, and leave prematurely if treated with anything less than candor and respect.[12]

Seek good data on their performance

If team members' current behavior towards you is not a good predictor of future performance, what is?

* In-depth discussions with them about what the group is doing right and what could be improved, what they do and do not like about their work, and what they could be doing for the business given opportunity
* Previous reviews, preferably coupled with a conversation with their former supervisors
* Available work metrics, thoughtfully interpreted

Use the gifts, not the gaps

From David Popler, experienced entrepreneur and executive: "Find out what they're great at, and free them to be great at it, rather than cramming people into predetermined spaces." You will have more success allocating work by team member strengths than coaching/prodding/training/incentivizing them to excel in boxes that suited the last crop of team members.

If you're in a large company and have yet to make an ally of your HR business partner, get on it. That person will be critical to gaining organizational support for your role changes.

Make the hard calls

Mike Thompson, experienced tech exec and new SVP at Lantiq, says "Nobody's expecting me to say the organization is fine. I find the A players and let them run for a while on their own. Then focus on B—and below—who do we keep. Then I look at how the chain of command is working—region VPs, managing regional managers, etc. When I'm satisfied that's working, then I work on strengthening the organization overall."

Ben Anderson, executive recruiter and senior-level advisor, says "what annoys boards and investors is someone who takes three quarters to sort out people decisions that were clear within a couple months. Many new CEOs are too slow to change the team, and performance suffers." When I ask first time CEOs what their big learnings have been—"I should have made the people changes faster" always ranks in the top three.

Hire very wisely

You're too busy right now to invest big blocks of time with top candidates for your openings? Think again. Who you hire broadcasts more about what's important to you than anything else.

Invest your time in making sure external or internal recruiting really understand who you need...not just experience but attitude and commitment. Let them vet candidates. Then invest time with the top candidates. Only you can make your best hire...and help them make a strong start!

---

12. Rob Goffee and Gareth Jones, *Clever: Leading Your Smartest, Most Creative People*, 1st ed., (Boston, MA: Harvard Business Press, 2009).

20 Communicate Early and Often

Human brains pay attention to what's recent, what's repeated, and what's communicated with passion and clarity. Memories of your email last week have faded in favor of whatever you talked about yesterday.

Keep it simple

Use a simple framework for presenting issues and your positions:

- Here's what I'm seeing
- Here's how I interpret it
- What am I missing?
- Here's what I think that means for us
- What do you think?

Explain your decisions. Especially when you're new, people are likely to misinterpret why you're doing what you're doing. Let them know what factors you weighted as priorities in making your decisions.

Speak up

Many new leaders communicate up far less than would be useful. "My boss is busy, and I don't want to waste her time." Of course not. Communicating with you should never be a waste of time.

Senior leaders in particular hate surprises. Socialize your ideas early, building momentum informally before presenting them as formal plans.

Here are conversations most bosses appreciate:

- This is what I'm aiming to accomplish by these dates. What do you think?
- Here's my plan for getting there. Anything to discuss on this?
- Here are our top three to five priorities, in order. Sound right?

- Here's how I'm developing my team. Your thoughts?
- Here are concerns I'm tracking and what I'm doing about them. Any input?
- What do you see changing across the company or industry that would be useful for me to know?
- Here's who I'm in touch with across the organization. Anyone else?
- Here's the help I'd like from you over the next month.

Recognize the change management challenges

Are you emphasizing new goals? Changing team members and roles? Asking people to do things differently? Recognize that you are now leading a change process, as well as leading your group. What seems like a modest change to you can be a big change to the people involved. Many people—including top performers—are change-averse, although few will say so to you. Do not underestimate the time, emotional energy, and communication required from you to make this successful.

Unless you are experienced at leading change initiatives, arrange support from HR, OD, or an external consultant or coach. Heck, if you are experienced at leading change, you've probably already placed that call for help.

Stay on message

Many leaders are reluctant to repeat themselves.[13] Consequently, they say it once or twice, maybe at a team meeting or in an email, intending their message to stand for all time.

When you care about something, say it often. Even better, ask about it often. For example, let's say you want your team to stay on top of supplier markets. Whenever a team member talks about product design, ask questions such as "Which suppliers could enable us to deliver on that?"

As you present—especially when you're presenting the same presentation over and over—make sure you're connecting with the people, not just delivering the information. Stay on message, but create a conversation that is tailored to each audience.

Build your brand

Presenting yourself and your messages consistently contributes to your "personal brand"—the qualities others associate with you.

When your peers are talking about you, what will they say? What will your team members say? Your boss? They're going to say something, so you may as well provide material that serves you and your goals.

When what you say is relevant, when you say it in a way that is notable, and when you act with sufficient consistency, you give focus to what others say about you. That's important, because news of your stellar qualities and impressive deeds will be seen as more credible coming from mouths other than your own.[14]

---

13. This distaste of repetition is typical of people who prefer iNtuition and Thinking on the Myers-Briggs Type Indicator. For more on personality type, see Appendix D.
14. Jeffrey Pfeffer, *Power: Why Some People Have It—and Others Don't*, (San Francisco, CA. Jossey-Bass, 2000).

Tell a Good Story

"If you want to shift beliefs and behavior in your organization, find or create stories."

Patrick Lencioni, author of *The Four Obsessions of an Extraordinary Executive*, has made a career of telling stories that move senior leaders to behave differently. Many of my interviewees mentioned Lencioni's books because the stories stuck. One of my clients, leader of a large corporate marketing group, even refers to the characters in his books by name as shorthand for behavior... "What would Rich do?" "Don't be Tom."[15]

Stories tell us what's important, how we do things around here, and when and how to skirt the rules. Decades of organizational psychology research show that stories are what people remember and repeat.[16]

Your first few months on the job are an especially powerful time to use language well. People want to know what the "new boss" is thinking, and they haven't started tuning you out yet. If what you say makes sense, helps them do their jobs, and inspires them, they may keep listening.

Make the most of metaphors

Often team members sidestep important issues because they don't know how to bring them up without sounding accusatory or complaining. As a new leader you can give fresh language to old

---

15. Patrick A. Lencioni, *The Four Obsessions of an Extraordinary Executive: A Leadership Fable*, (New York, NY: HarperCollins, 2010).
16. J. Martin and M. Powers, "Organizational Stories: More Vivid and Persuasive than Quantitative Data," *Psychological Foundations of Organizational Behavior*, 2nd ed., (Barry Straw. Glenview, IL: Scott Foresman, 1983).

problems. When one of my clients entered a company that was slipping on execution, he started asking about "promises"—"What promises have you made about this?" Execution got back on track.

In business, we use metaphor constantly. "We need to divide and conquer"; "How can we reel in our top prospects?"; and, my least favorite, "Will the dogs eat the dog food?"

When Kent Thiry took over near-bankrupt Total Renal Care, he put language at the center of the change. He called the company a "village" and employees "citizens." He convened 700 citizens to rename the company, which became "DaVita"—meaning *giver of life*. Ten years of culture-driven change have made DaVita profitable in a very tough market.[17]

Choose powerful interpretations

Every view of something is an interpretation. We interpret events and people as good/bad, hopeful/scary, smart/foolish, etc., against our own backdrop of cultural belief and personal history.

Infinite interpretations are available for every situation. Nevertheless, people usually assume that the first interpretation their minds kick out is an accurate description of what's really going on. And, as soon as they speak to that description, that IS what's going on.

Since you've got to choose some interpretations for your experiences, you might as well choose powerful ones. I define a powerful interpretation as one that enables you to take wise action.

When a client stepped in to lead a high-visibility regional agency, she saw that city departments held the critical manpower. Unfortunately, city officials paid little attention to her agenda. She could have interpreted their uncollaborative behavior as inevitable, given differing priorities; based on this interpretation, she could have decided to lower her expectations or strong-arm the cities through budget or media. Instead, she chose to view their intransigence as a reasonable response to years of inconsistent agency behavior and adversarial meeting formats. With this insight, she guided the group to revamp meetings, and she focused her team on communicating consistently.

Talk usefully to yourself

The most influential conversations are those we have with ourselves.

What you say about yourself—if only to yourself—powerfully shapes your own sense of possibilities. Cognitive framing—how you describe a situation to yourself—is your most important lever for making change.

As you become more aware of the stories you tell and the metaphors you use, you see your own implicit view of the situation. With this insight, you can see more possibilities and make more strategic decisions.

---

17. Jeffrey Pfeffer, "Kent Thiry and DaVita," *Harvard Business Review*, February 23, 2006.

22

Bring Value to Any Room

"Your attention alone will be valuable."

How do you show up? In other words, what comes in the room when you walk in? Good data, clarity, courage? Or unexamined assumptions, anxiety, and blame?

There are many ways to bring value to a room—here are a few that are especially appropriate for new leaders.

Offer insight

I've found that the most influential person in a meeting is usually the one who is most clear about his/her own thinking and about decisions that are needed from the group.

Prepare by capturing your thinking and questions about the topic at hand in what I call The Crucial One-Pager. It may be a sequenced set of questions, a draft of decision criteria, a matrix, a process flow diagram, whatever. The point is you've got a point...or at least you know what questions you want to raise to the group. Whether you choose to talk about what you've put on that page, you've set your brain in motion.

If your thinking is too befuddled to allow you to prepare few bullets or a simple diagram, STOP! Before marching fuzzyheaded into that meeting, step back and think.

- What's the one message you want to make sure people walk away with?
- What are the most compelling reasons they should believe the message?
- What evidence do you have that those reasons hold water?
- Where might your thinking be incomplete, and what could you learn in this meeting?

Map it

When you're struggling to communicate something in words, consider whether a simple diagram could make your point clear. Brain research confirms that our minds hold images more easily than verbal or written text.[18] By picking up a marker and mapping the points people are making, you can check that you yourself understand the reasoning. Plus, once an idea is represented on paper or a whiteboard, others can more easily follow and usefully contribute to the group effort.

Say it

Says Mike Thompson, SVP of Lantiq, "I'm frank right from the start. Hidden agendas are what freak people out."

Research on teams shows the more broadly known a piece of data is, the more likely to be discussed in team meetings.[19] In other words, people—especially those with lower status in the group—tend to sit on disconfirming data and unique insights.

If you've prepared as we've discussed and you've listened to other views, trust you'll have something valuable to say. If you're ambivalent, say so. There's information in ambivalence. Resist the temptation either to ramble or remain silent. Instead, simply offer the best of your thinking..."I think plan X best meets our objectives, but I'm hesitant because of Y. What are your thoughts on how we can solve Y?"

Pay attention

Maybe the easiest way to add value is to be quiet, mute your phone, and give the other person your full attention. Your attention alone will be valuable. You can also help them clarify their own thoughts by offering your understanding of what they've said. You can ask questions. You can offer possibilities you see.

In a larger meeting, you can be helpful by listening thoughtfully, inviting varied points of view, and expressing brief and sincere appreciation. I'm not suggesting you do this routinely—that will come off as shtick or manipulation. I am suggesting that you can add value even before you have deep content knowledge.

---

18. David Rock, *Your Brain at Work: Strategies for Overcoming Distraction, Regaining Focus, and Working Smarter All Day Long.* 1 ed. (New York, NY: HarperCollins, 2009).
19. Gwen M. Wittenbaum and Ernest S. Park, "The Collective Preference for Shared Information," *Current Directions in Psychological Science,* 10 no. 2 (April 2001): 70–73.

23 Balance Curiosity, Advice, and Silence

"You might just close your mouth sometimes and see what happens."

You've got to figure out when to ask, when to tell, and when to shut up. That can be a whole lot harder than it sounds. Three top reasons new leaders fail, according to a recent large study, are intimidating others, jumping to conclusions, and reacting negatively to criticism.[20]

When in doubt, get curious

Think team members are screwing up? Be curious about what they think they're supposed to be doing. Think a peer is subtly attacking you? Be curious about his/her intent. Think your boss is withholding opinions? Be curious about how you can show your openness to feedback. And so on.

When you're truly curious and open, you cannot at the same time be browbeating people, forming hasty conclusions, and reacting defensively. So, at a minimum, curiosity will keep you from common traps. Even better, curiosity will help you find out what's really going on. And, as you role model curiosity, your team is likely to become better prepared.

Make your thinking transparent

I bet you've seen something like this...

New Leader: I know you all need a decision about when we're launching the FlubDub product line. I've decided: November 15.

Team: "OK, Boss."

---

20. Jack Zenger, Joe Folkman, and Kurt Sandholtz. "Five Insights From Leadership Research," July, 2009, http://www.workforce.com/section/11/feature/26/52/35/index_printer.html

Team member **A** walks away thinking: "Wow, new boss just doesn't trust us to deliver in September like we originally planned."

Team member **B** is thinking: "That guy is pushing us like dogs. With the production problems at the new plant, it's gonna be hell to meet that date."

Team member **C** is thinking: "So I guess he's not interested in ScrubBub product, because we were going to launch that in early November, and we can't handle two launches. Guess it's time to pull that plug."

Team member **D** is thinking: "This guy must think the FlubDub team is hot stuff, if he's driving to a date that soon. Sounds like he can't be bothered with our existing line. Guess I should start looking for a new job."

If you do not explain the reasoning behind your decisions, your colleagues' brains will be happy to make stuff up. That's just what brains do. As one of my interviews, an experienced technology executive, said: "I make sure people don't have to spend time figuring out what I'm really thinking."

Give advice sparingly

Why sparingly? After all, you were hired to lead this group because you know so much, right?

Not so fast. People become used to asking your advice rather than thinking. You become used to playing what Nilofer Merchant beautifully calls "Chief of Answers."[21] Pretty soon, your group effectively has one brain, yours, which will become quite tired very soon.

So, what could you do the next time you're tempted to give advice?

* Ask the person what he sees.
  Choosing what to notice is one of the most powerful decisions we make. However, attention is frequently aimed by habit and old fears. By sharpening awareness of what we do and the results we create, we can make more useful choices. Often, from awareness itself new behaviors emerge.
* Offer your observations.
  Perhaps you'll discover that each of you focuses on different aspects of the situation. Just learning where you place your attention and what you notice may give the person some additional perspective on the issue.
* Help them explore their options.
  Sometimes our own minds are a pretty tiny space to spread out big issues, gain perspective, and re-chart our course. In conversation, you give ideas a bigger work table, hold up their mental map for a closer look, and consider together the risks and rewards of potential actions.

Consider silence

You might just close your mouth and see what happens. In the presence of your attentive silence, people might find answers to their own problems.

---

21. Nilofer Merchant, *The New How: Creating Business Solutions Through Collaborative Strategy*, 1 ed. (Sebastopol, CA.: O'Reilly Media, Inc., 2010).

Part V
Create Your Management System

You're hitting your stride.

Now, make the time to turn your tactics into systems. Define your processes for managing risk, communicating up/down/sideways, managing performance, and developing talent.

- Rule 24: Make Your Own Metrics
- Rule 25: Catalog Risks and Start Mitigating
- Rule 26: Run Unmissable Meetings
- Rule 27: Adjust Your Approach
- Rule 28: Launch 1:1s that Actually Drive Performance
- Rule 29: Make the Most of Screwups
- Rule 30: Grow More Leaders
- Rule 31: Call in the Experts

24 Make Your Own Metrics

"Becoming the person with good numbers is a handy addition to any personal brand."

If your car's speedometer displayed temperature rather than speed, combined your speed with those of nearby cars, or gave you just your average speed for the preceding month, you'd get it fixed, right?

Or, would you just "go with your gut"? Then say, "But Officer, it felt about right, and besides my broken speedometer said I was doing fine!"

You can't drive well with a lousy dashboard, and you can't lead well with lousy numbers, either.

Do it yourself

Rather than relying on or complaining about your company's insufficient reports, make your own dashboard.

Identify three to five business imperatives for your group. Typically, your imperatives will include something about...

- Delivering tremendous value to your customers
- Creating outputs
- Partnering in and out of the organization in ways that create even more value
- Developing your team to be ever more capable of doing all of this

For each imperative, come up with several smart measures that indicate your group's degree of progress and success. Having created top-level dashboards for multi-billion dollar companies and tiny nonprofits, I've learned to start with the right questions, rather than reach for whatever data is handy. The key questions are always, "What will give us early warning as to how we're doing?" and "What will show us the key factors driving performance up or down?"

Here's what to look for in choosing measures:

- Select leading rather than lagging indicators, as much as possible (How many customers clicked on the service contract page and the percentage that bought a contract, rather than service contract revenue)
- Pull from data you can find or reasonably estimate monthly
- Make sure you can learn the precise origins of the data and understand their weaknesses
- Look to a variety of sources, incorporating market as well as company data
- Create new data streams when needed. Tally something at the front lines. Negotiate with an upstream unit for earlier data. Make an index from public financials
- Ask for lots of input on potential metrics, especially about data quality, ease of pulling data, interpretations, and credibility
- Choose at least some of the metrics to be especially credible to your team, executives, other functions, and even customers

Put together a monthly dashboard

At the simplest: Make a spreadsheet, one page for each month, with your measures as rows, organized by imperative. Columns may include this month's data, last month's data or three-month rolling average, and this time last year, whatever you consider relevant. Include a column to color green, yellow, or red and one for any critical notes on reasons or data.

If you're new to thinking about measures, there's plenty of material online about balanced scorecards, executive dashboards, etc. See the resources section (http://ideashape.com/leadstartbook/resources) for this book. Make a good start, commit to doing it, and improve as you go.

Think about implications

Block two hours each month to consider what this means and what more you need to know to interpret and make use of the data. Gather with team members and consult your best peers. Ask:

- What's in flux and what's stable? Why?
- What are we doing that creates these results?
- What's really going on?
- What happens if we keep doing what we've been doing?
- What are the highest-value changes we could make? And, what are the implications for risk?
- What metrics would be even more revealing than current ones?

Communicate!

You've got the goods now. Becoming the person with good numbers is a handy addition to any personal brand. More important, you'll use your deeper understanding of the metrics to focus your team on what matters. In addition, as you become a devoted student of the sometimes unobvious relationships between cause and effect, you become a more valuable strategic thought-partner to your leadership and your customers.

25

Catalog Risks and Start Mitigating

"Look for the problems that are sending 'weak' distress signals."

Unless you're running an undersea mining rig, chances are no one will ask to see your risk mitigation plan. And, don't count on getting brownie points for telling people you have one. Your peers might call you Doomsday Dave, and most of your team will not care and may resent the extra work to prep for unlikely events.

So, why do it?

- Your savviest customers (external and internal) will care how you're handling risks that directly impact uptime and delivery.
- When (not if) something bad happens, you may look like a hero instead of a fool. The first few months of a new job is a costly time to look like a fool.
- You're the leader, and that means you're thinking ahead to possible events, options, and outcomes. If you don't lead this effort for your group, don't expect anyone to do it for you. Protecting the future of your organization starts with you.

Determine risks and mitigation

Some companies have fancy systems with sophisticated probability calculations. Your risk management database could be as simple as a Google Doc with a few columns:

- The risk
- Probability of occurrence (1/month, 1/year, 1/decade?)
- Likely damage to business ($ order of magnitude)
- Early warning signals
- Potential avoidance/mitigation actions, with likely effectiveness
- Current actions to avoid/mitigate, with specific responsibilities

Start with what's smoldering

You already know what's on fire...that's what's filling your inbox. Start populating your database by looking for the problems that are sending "weak" distress signals yet your experience tells you could have big negative impacts.

Launch a systematic process to catalog risks

Start with a framework of types of risks:

* Customers—Change in decision-makers? Bankruptcies?
* Suppliers—Input scarcities? Delivery interruptions?
* Financial markets—Credit tightening? Currency fluctuations?
* Industry developments—Competitor strategic shifts? New players?
* Political environment—Regulatory pressures? Interest groups?
* Internal risk—M & A activity upstream? Tech rollouts?
* People risk—Skills? Recruiting success rate? Retention?
  (you will probably need to keep a private supplemental analysis)

Once you've refined the framework for your business, invite your team for a risk identification kickoff, which oddly can be a really fun meeting. Low-tech, it's flip chart and stickies; higher tech, you're all directly populating a collaborative database. Team members usually come away from the meeting thinking much more broadly about the business and more creatively about upside opportunities, as well as downside risks.

Assess risks more thoroughly

My experience is that you'll be more successful separating the process of cataloging risks from assessing them. Typically, to start you'll want to have the full group cataloging risks and then have specific team members, in pairs or trios, assess an assigned category of risks and enter information in the system.

Charge each mini-team to do a "lightning round" of assessing their risk areas followed by a more thorough assessment and an ongoing process to monitor and update risk ratings.

After the "lightning round," it's time to prioritize. Draw a 2 x 2 matrix on a chart, placing risks according to probability and potential damage. Color-code for how hard or easy to mitigate the risk. Now you, ideally with a couple of experienced team members, take a look at the picture, consider the benefits against the cost of mitigation, and figure out which risks are worth addressing now with which mitigation strategies.

26 Run Unmissable Meetings

"You want to develop the practice of encouraging dissent at the meeting, instead of in the hall later."

Want to win the hearts of your team? Stop wasting their time.

Do away with the narcolepsy-inducing stuff—updates, rehashes, talking people through templates. This can be handled via shared files and workspace technology; Google Docs is free, no excuses.

Run fascinating meetings

What makes meetings fascinating? Crucial content, latest news, big questions, real points of view and dissent, vital decisions, and determining who gets to do what. Add a dash of good humor, sincere appreciation, and friendly competition, and voilà! You have must-make meetings.

Go through all the meetings your team is used to enduring. Kick them up to this level or take them off the docket. Of course, not all issues require the full team. Ask for huddles with the right people on specific issues. Make full-team meetings short and powerful.

Ace the logistics

I was invited to join the volunteer leadership team of a nonprofit with lousy meetings. The agenda was mostly ignored, experienced members shut down important queries with "that's not relevant," decisions were declared without checking for dissent, and follow-up actions were noted only haphazardly. When I called attention to this, the officers said "we're so effective we don't need meeting procedures." I declined to waste more of my time with this team.

Nail the basics:

- Create a timed agenda and send it in advance. Ask for any changes to the agenda at the beginning. Always include some time at end for new issues.
- Make sure the crucial people are there or conferenced in.
- Set the expectation of no side conversations or techno-surfing. When you're there, you're focused. For longer meetings, set aside breaks for sidebars and checking email.
- Have someone capture key data, insights, and to-dos (what, by whom, by when) and send to participants immediately after the meeting.
- At the end of most meetings, run a quick plus/delta, reviewing what worked that we want to do again, what should we do differently next time.

Ann Blocker, healthcare strategist and COO, used these processes to improve and shorten her monthly all-hands operations meetings. At the end of each meeting, she asked her team what worked for them about the meeting and what didn't. Within a couple months, what had been a meeting with lots of telling (and yawning) became a brief, edge-of-your-seat exchange on the most critical decisions the team needed to make.

Make it easy to offer ideas

If you've teed up big issues and you've got the right people in the room, properly caffeinated, there will be more thoughts in people's heads than airtime to hear them.

Capture these thoughts! For starters, place stacks of 3 X 5 post-its around the table. Ask people to jot down thoughts, one per post-it, as they have them. These can be arranged on a flip chart on the fly as needed and/or handed to the person who has responsibility for that issue.

For strategic or contentious issues, large meetings, and/or when you want to be a full participant, consider professional facilitation.

Invite dissent

Ask explicitly for data or thoughts that argue against the position developing in the meeting.

You want to develop the practice of encouraging dissent at the meeting, instead of in the hall later. When you're offering your point of view, ask, "What am I missing?" "How would_____department look at this?" "What would our competitors ask?"

Do not rely on the same people to play "devil's advocates"; that tends to lock-in their reputations as "naysayers" and take others off the hook for critical thinking. Rather, you want everyone to participate in offering the best info and insight they're sitting on, for and against any proposal.

Adjust Your Approach

"You'd be surprised—they're all individual countries," President Ronald Reagan said of South America. Seems some leaders are surprised their team members are all individuals, too.

Lighten up on talking about "your leadership style" and think more about what you could do that would be truly useful for your team members and colleagues.

Adjust for their competence and confidence

The leadership model most mentioned as helpful by my interviewees also happens to be one of my favorites: Situational Leadership II, from the Ken Blanchard Companies.[22] This simple-yet-powerful framework helps leaders diagnose each team member's need for support and direction on critical tasks—and adjust their management accordingly. This body of work is also a terrific resource for having development conversations with your team members. You can use the same concepts to identify the direction and support that would help you succeed in your role. Take a course, if you can, on how to use this model well.

Adjust for their personalities and preferred ways of work

When a highly-competent marketing VP I had coached moved to a different company, she was in for a shock. Her initial meetings fell flat. Used to an extraverted team that alternately interrupted her,

---

22. Ken Blanchard. "The Ken Blanchard Companies, Situational Leadership II," http://www.kenblanchard.com/

argued and cheered, she was shocked that her new group listened, nodded, and left. Knowing something about personality type differences, she quickly deduced that her new team was not suffering from aphasia, fear, or stupidity. They were predominantly introverted, with many types that value respect for senior levels over love of debate.

I've developed an easy model to help you remember three useful ways to be flexible to differences:

* Appreciate: always look for value in the differences people bring to teamwork
  ("Great! She's tracking the details.")
* Adapt: sometimes adjust your behavior to help other people get what they need to be more productive
  ("I can provide more detail for her than I do for others.")
* Adopt: occasionally draw on less-used/less-comfortable behaviors so you can be more effective
  ("For this budget meeting, I need to be on top of the details.")

Myers-Briggs was mentioned often by my interviewees as a useful framework for valuing personality differences at work. I agree. For more, see Appendix D.

Make reasonable accommodations to respect their preferred ways of working. Says Ann Blocker, experienced COO, "In our second or third meeting, I ask them: what do you want—from me, in your environment—that helps you to be successful? I usually give them examples: Quiet work time/space? Time to read background information before a meeting? Makes sense to do what I can to help them be productive."

Create a diversity-positive zone

Nina Bhatti, Principal Scientist at HP Labs, made a strong case for a leader's role in respecting diversity; you can hear her remarks as I interviewed her for the Weekly Leader Podcast.[23] She spoke about making a team environment where people can feel safe to be who they are. With a great story about dressing down a boss who taunted the vegetarian on her team with offers of burger dinners, she called on leaders to stand up for individual differences. One of my mentors in strategy consulting, Kathryn Clubb, speaks of "deep regard" as a pillar of leadership.

Diversity of all sorts—ethnic, educational, geographic, personality, age—is valuable to an organization only when people feel free to bring those differences to work. Forming a team of diverse individuals is just the beginning. The real value comes when your team members use their varying experiences to think divergently. Your job is to make it safe for people to show up with their differences and to make the most of their different perspectives to drive innovation.

---

23. Pam Fox Rollin, "Weekly Leader Podcast Episode 43 with Nina Bhatti, Principal Scientist, HP Labs," http://weeklyleader.net/2010/weekly-leader-podcast-episode-43-with-nina-bhatti-principle-scientist-hp-labs/

Launch 1:1s that Actually Drive Performance

"When you have to choose between your agenda and their agenda, favor their agenda, so you learn what they're thinking."

There's no substitute for private, thoughtful, uninterrupted, minimally-structured time with each team member. This is especially critical in your first three to six months of working together.

Commit to each of your people

You will be spending what feels like a ridiculous amount of time with each of your team members. Right, this isn't sustainable, yet it's too early to know who really needs time with you, how often and how long.

If you have many direct reports, it usually works better to meet for a shorter time (20 to 30 minutes) each one to two weeks than to let it go too long between meetings. When you have to choose between your agenda and their agenda, favor their agenda, so you learn what they're thinking.

Offer a simple format

For scheduled meetings, ask your team members to come ready to talk about

- their top few priorities (this week, this quarter)
- challenges/obstacles they're encountering and how they're handling them
- opportunities they notice in their role or for the team
- what would be helpful from you.

From time to time, set aside time to ask about the big picture—what they enjoy and don't, what they want to learn next, how they see their career developing.

Achieve "mind meld" on priorities

Nothing is more frustrating for team members than breaking their backs on a project that you didn't bother to tell them is no longer a priority. Your greatest power as a leader is to focus your people to work on the right things.

What are the chances that "complete product launch plan" means the exact same thing to you as it does to your reports? Achieve clarity about success, starting with asking them to describe what the project will look like at the end and the next milestone. When you need to suggest a different approach, check for understanding: "What is it you're taking away from our conversation?"

Come curious. If your staffer highlights a priority not on your list, ask about it. I know this sounds obvious...check to make sure you're actually asking instead of telling.

Keep your hands off the wheel

You're asking them about challenges and opportunities because you want to find out what's going on, see how they navigate it, and coach them when appropriate. Do NOT take over their challenges, and certainly not their opportunities.

If you believe that a team member has encountered a problem too big for him to solve, or an opportunity too great, ask more. If your concerns remain, share them in a way that invites the team member to think it through, perhaps with you or another team member as a thought partner. To raise your game at coaching, check the online resources for this Rule.

Nail your next steps

As you ask about obstacles and opportunities, keep a list of actions that would be useful from you or others. At the end of each issue or your meeting, go through the list together to figure out the next step, asking for their recommendations and offering your thoughts as needed. If you're working with someone highly committed and capable at that task area, you may need to confirm just the couple actions you'll take.

Once the 1:1 is over, you're role-modeling the follow-up you expect from your team. Make sure you accomplish your follow-up to-dos promptly and confirm back to your team member.

Finally, I know you're busy, especially now, but do show up for 1:1s. When I interview teams that aren't working, one of the most common factors I hear is "My boss often cancels our 1:1s." When you absolutely can't keep a meeting, reach out fast and reschedule at a time that works well for your team member.

Make the Most of Screwups

If you're a leader long enough, something will go badly wrong. Maybe a project will come in over budget or perhaps your product launch will flop. If you're lucky, the grand failures will come after enough time under your belt to have the credibility to survive the bump. Rather than counting on luck, let's see how you and your team can survive screw-ups.

Ban the blame, and lead the learning

One of my first—and best—bosses was John Donahoe, now CEO of eBay. At the time, he was a just a couple of years out of business school and a new manager at Bain & Company. Nevertheless, he inspired loyalty and high performance by pulling his teams together to solve problems. He quickly put a stop to bickering: "Let's get the learning out of this, and move on."

When screw-ups happen, ban the blame. (OK, give your team five minutes of moaning if they must.) Then, what are we learning from this? Is this lesson now a hypothesis to test or a new law of nature?

Also important, what do we *not* want to take away from this experience? We've all worked with teams that were bogged down in the minefields of "we tried that once, got burned, and we'll never do it again"...where "it" encompasses huge fields of action like "market directly to end customers" or "measure team performance."

Build relationships as you recover

As a terrific mentor in my corporate strategy consulting days told me, "There are two times to delight your customer—before you screw up and after you screw up."

Your customers—internal as well as external—expect error-free delivery. Your best customers also want a great partner: someone who will tell the truth, learn from stumbles, solve problems creatively, and take responsibility for making it right. Seeing your team recover well from a stumble can strengthen customer relationships rather than damage them.

Remember your team will be looking to you, especially the first couple times things go wrong. If you stay focused on serving your customer and improving the system, you're teaching your team what to do. If you hide problems, shade truth, and lay blame, expect more of the same.

Figure out what went wrong

You are going to be held accountable for answering the question of "what went wrong." It's not always an easy process—this type of reverse engineering can take as much time or more as your initial planning did. It's sometimes worth it in the long run, both in terms of accountability and prevention.

When a problem arises, reach out right away—to your team members, customers. Express your commitment to making things right, then fire up your curiosity and interview people as if for a case study. Save any non-urgent fixes until you and your team have developed a solid picture of the factors that contributed to the problem; consider faulty processes, limited frames of thinking, poor information, overly-simplistic metrics and incentives, even your lack of experience in picking up early signs of trouble.

Repair the short-term damage, share the learnings across the team, and improve your processes. You leave the screw-up with processes and team stronger than before. Onward!

When YOU screw up

All the above applies to you, too. Say you were wrong, make repairs, and explain how you're going to ensure that it doesn't happen again.

I interviewed a colleague I had mentored early in my career, who now has succeeded across several C-level roles. He said, "I make maybe 100 decisions a day. If I'm right on 90 of them, that's pretty good."

Grow More Leaders

> "If you develop a reputation as a great boss, you'll have a steady supply of great people who want to work for you."

Your job is to make other people even more successful. (If you don't like that part of the job, don't lead.)

See leaders everywhere

One of the benefits of doing (really good) team building work with Myers-Briggs or similar tools is that you see and challenge your own assumptions about different sorts of people.

Very often, I hear "I have great people on my team, but few potential leaders." As we look more closely, we usually discover

- High-capability introverts who people assumed didn't want to take leadership roles (wrong!)
- Transfers from other groups who aren't totally competent in their current role (yet may have great potential to lead, especially cross functional initiatives)
- Others who don't "look like" the current leadership team—different education, different social class, too old, too young, etc.

People tend to trust those who appear most like themselves. If you want to become great at grooming talent, know your biases and make an effort to challenge them.

Become curious about their skills and capabilities

Years ago, I was tapped to co-lead a big change initiative for a health plan. Eight people from across the organization had been picked to join the core team—including first-level supervisors, union-member workers, and others who didn't see themselves (or each other) as leaders. Trust wasn't there, and our start was slow and awkward.

Somehow, I thought to ask, "I'm curious—what do each of us do really well that we don't usually have a chance to do in our current job?" As people started to talk, first hesitantly, then with enthusiasm, the atmosphere transformed. We learned the admin was a rock star organizer of sports leagues in her community. We discovered the actuary loved to write. We began to see how much capability we had in the room—more than we suspected, just from knowing job titles. This group pulled together as a team and succeeded at leading the organization to change.

Craft roles for success

Adobe CEO Shantanu Narayen says, "If I can complement people's strengths by surrounding them with people who can complement their areas of weakness, that's probably a better recipe for success than trying to say, 'O.K., you need to change.'"[24]

If you were to guess what percentage of their day your team members spent doing what they're brilliant at, would that even rise above 50%? Clients I ask typically estimate 25–40%, and they know that's not good enough. From a successful entrepreneur I interviewed: "Pains me to see people locked into their roles, instead of growing into their capability."

Could you imagine, with redesigned roles and adequate support, your people spending 80% of their day using their strengths?

Champion your people

- Bring them to important meetings, showcasing them where appropriate. Make sure you prepare them in advance and debrief together after.
- Invite them into your network. Help them plug into civic or business circles in your community.
- Speak well of your team members. Make a point to remember specific examples of wise actions, high levels of customer service, effective risk management, and so forth, and include those in your conversations with peers and up.

Many new leaders shine the spotlight away from their team members for fear of having their best people poached by more powerful peers. Yes, that can happen. However, look at it this way: if you develop a reputation as a great boss, you'll have a steady supply of great people who want to work for you. In addition, one of those poached stars may become your peer or even boss some day, and they usually remember how great you are.

---

24. Adam Bryant, "Connecting the Dots Isn't Enough," July 18, 2009, http://www.nytimes.com/2009/07/19/business/19corner.html

31

Call in the Experts

"Do you cut your own hair?"

If this job is big enough to be interesting to you, you won't be able to do it all yourself—not if you want time for a life. Focus on doing what you do best and find support for the rest.

What tasks can you offload?

What are the tasks you need to do over the next three and six months? Bucket them by skills (and in some cases relationships) needed.

Now, let's focus on you. Pull out the list of strengths and weaknesses that you compiled as you read Rules 11 and 12. Which of these tasks represent your "sweet spot" of skill and expertise? Your energy, time and experience are best spent focusing on them.

How well (and/or fast) could someone else to do the tasks? Does being successful with the task require relationships and insight that only you have, or is the task something discrete that could be accomplished by someone else? Write performance reviews for my directs? Not likely. Write a PowerPoint summary of market opportunities? Sure.

You may find it useful to make a spreadsheet with these columns and ratings of 3, 2, and 1 (3 as high fit and 1 as low fit):

• Type of task
• Fit with my skills/knowledge?
• Fit with energy/time?
• Central to my role/relationships?

Might this be a development opportunity for a team member?

On work that really can't be contracted out but doesn't fit into your schedule either, find a team member who's ready to step up. It's also a great chance for you to coach an emerging leader. Plus, the next time the task needs to be done, you'll have someone prepped.

Add cheap help

Do you need quick research? A database set up to analyze your metrics? A presentation to communicate the ideas you've already developed? Are you spending a lot of time keying in data or documenting processes? These tasks are perfect for an intern, temp, or virtual assistant. Remember this person will need good directions and supervision. Bonus points for finding an individual contributor on your team to supervise the temp: coach your team member to supervise, and you build skills that stay in your group.

Figure out where experts can help

Do you cut your own hair? Fix your car's computer?

When personal tasks require expertise you don't have (and have no reason or time to develop), you get help. Nevertheless, people in organizations often take on tasks they have no business doing.

Highly-regarded leaders I interviewed hired experts within their first few months to

- Analyze geographic expansion opportunities
- Upgrade website capabilities
- Evaluate suppliers—existing and potential
- Facilitate strategic offsites
- Coach team members they promoted
- Guide the downsizing or hiring processes
- Train team members on new technology

Gain organizational support (or invisibility)

Not everyone up, across, and down the organizational chart will appreciate your sensible plan for matching tasks with talents. Recognize and handle any legitimate concerns about confidentiality, intellectual property, or knowledge transfer. Once you've satisfied those concerns, successful leaders handle further resistance to outsourcing by overcoming or avoiding it:

- Persuade doubters of the wisdom of your plan. Highlight subbing out as an important opportunity for people/team development or contract management experience. Offer to make this a pilot project and share your process and learnings with other units.
- Pay contractors from your discretionary budget or keep fees small enough to avoid triggering any onerous vendor management processes. Keep in mind that you are accountable for your use of organizational resources, so use good judgment.

Part VI
Stay Smart

This one's all on you.

If you neglect to set targets, hire staff, and meet with them, your boss or team will remind you.

If you neglect to stay smart, seek feedback, and build your network, no one is likely to mention the gap. You'll just become less and less valuable.

After you've navigated the first couple months, calendar time each week to lift your head up out of the day to day. Build your insight about the future of the business as diligently as you manage current work.

- Rule 32: Strengthen Your Strategic Point of View
- Rule 33: Stay Current and Capable
- Rule 34: Model Healthy Paranoia
- Rule 35: Ferret Out Feedback
- Rule 36: Build Your Industry Presence

32 Strengthen Your Strategic Point of View

You start your new job fully aware of where your company's been in recent years and knowledgeable about where it's going. You're current on industry trends and where your firm stands in the marketplace. Don't lose your edge.

Keep your POV fresh

I love the story about Gordon Moore and Andy Grove during a tough spell at Intel wondering if they got canned, what a new CEO would do. They decided to walk out the door, walk back in, and do it themselves.[25]

The advantage of being an outsider is fresh eyes. You can see routines that survive often for no reason other than "that's the way we've always done it." Set aside time to bring your mind back into the outsider mindset and examine priorities and projects from that perspective. Ask yourself how a smart business rival would react if they knew of your plans. Would your competitor laugh, or would they rush Product Development into overdrive to launch first?

Create your informal Board of Advisors

Look for people of wisdom and integrity who understand who you are and what you're creating, who delight in your success, who enjoy conversing with you, and who have expertise beyond yours. People with no connection to your industry can be even more valuable because they see dynamics invisible from up close, and they have no horse in the race.

---

25. Tim Jackson, *Inside Intel: Andrew Grove and the Rise of the World's Most Powerful Chip Company*, 1 ed. (New York, NY: Dutton, 1997).

My clients have built their informal advisory boards from former class-mates, ex-colleagues, and friends of friends. Often those who've known you longest know you best. They've seen how your personality directs your thinking and can remind you of past incidents where similar thinking led you down a wise or unwise path.

A fast and effective way to create your cabinet is to reciprocate, perhaps creating a group of six to eight people from adjacent fields who talk regularly as a sounding board for each other's ideas. You can invite input as a group or one-on-one, regularly or occasionally, in person, by email, or by conference call.

Befriend academics, policy wonks, and good thinkers

Remember the professor who wrote that article you thought was brilliant? Or the think-tank director whose quotes in a magazine article spurred you to think about your business in a new light? Or that guy down the hall at your first job who was so thoughtful and well-informed?

Most of these folks are delighted to have a real-world leader interested in applying their thoughts. Reach out to them. Ask them for a short phone chat about their latest work of interest. When you're in their city, ask them to coffee or lunch.

Keep in touch, and repay them with meaningful visibility. Reference their work in your blog. When your company invites thought-leaders as paid speakers, include them. Ask them about the future directions of their work, and connect them with useful contacts.

Update your Strategic One-Pager

If you made your Strategic One-Pager (as described in Rule #4), you know how valuable it is to have a well-considered point of view. Don't let it get stale! Take all that good conversation with advisors and good thinkers, add your smarts, and freshen your POV.

By now, you're ready for more than one page. Determine the three to five critical decision/action areas for your business, and write a one-pager for each.

For one of my clients, managing director of a consulting firm, these aspects of the business are strategically critical:
* How we hire, develop, manage, path our talent
* How we develop and spread know-how across teams and offices
* Why prospects choose us over the competition
* How we keep spending at prudent levels while growing rapidly

Which aspects of your business are strategically critical?

What's your well-considered point of view?

33 Stay Current and Capable

"Adjust your media diet over time as your priorities change, and sources wax and wane."

If you read every relevant article, research report, and blog about your industry, function, customers, and markets...you'd never have time to do your job.

What you need are clear priorities, great funnels, and easy ways to access, use, and store the best content.

Drive your own development

You want to stay smart about where you're going, not just where you are. So make the effort to think through: What might you be doing a couple of years from now? For the top two to three possibilities, what would be handy to know? What technologies should you gain experience with? Who would be useful to know?

Turn this into an organized set of issues you want to stay on top of and networks you want to build. Then give yourself a time budget for keeping up-to-date—say half-hour a day plus a couple of hours each week for building relationships and doing some in-depth reading.

Scan your best sources every day

First, make your best sources come to you. I'm blown away by dear colleagues here in Silicon Valley who still haven't figured out how to feed RSS to their email, make a Twitter list of custom news-feeds, receive newsbreaks on key customers and competitors, or listen to podcasts on their smart-phone. Enlist your most techie friend, and get on it!

Then, develop the habit of scanning the sources daily for your priority learning areas. Soon, this will become efficient, as you figure out which bloggers, columnists, podcasters, etc. give you the best content for your time. Adjust your media diet over time as your priorities change and sources wax and wane.

While some argue that there's no point saving content in an era when everything is searchable, I find it helpful to keep links to articles that are especially insightful on priority issues. I like EverNote; find something that works for you.[26]

Find colleagues who stretch you

When early-career clients ask me for one change that will accelerate their success, I recommend they upgrade the circle they turn to for perspective and advice. Instead of commiserating or swapping ignorance with people who know pretty much what you know, find people with other areas of expertise and build mutually valuable relationships. Have lunch with people in other groups, other companies, other social circles. Some highly capable colleagues are helpful, others aren't. Find those who are.

You are looking for colleagues who will tell you the truth as they know it and connect you with good people. Beyond that, you are looking for people who will challenge you to go beyond your comfort zone. For example, two weeks into my post-MBA start at Accenture, I asked a dozen people to review a technology strategy backgrounder I was preparing for leaders at Kaiser Permanente. Two colleagues, Lesley Frana and Joseph Villa, responded with valuable comments. They encouraged me to talk with them, which of course I did. That conversation significantly raised my game, not only about the topic, but also about challenging people to advance their thinking. What I learned in that conversation has served me for years.

Consider joining or creating a learning community.

Think of a competency you're developing or a field where you want to keep current. What if, instead of going it alone, you pooled your questions and learnings with others? It's easy to manage your own interest group or learning community. The hard part can be finding sharp, savvy people you trust, especially if confidentiality is an issue. One approach is to ask your current network who they would contact to learn more about that issue. In reaching out to experts, you may discover an existing learning community. If not, I've found that experts are often delighted to participate in a learning community as long as you make excellent use of their time and help them keep their finger on the pulse of current developments.

---

26. http://www.evernote.com

34 Model Healthy Paranoia

We had a saying when I worked at the strategy consultancy Bain & Company, "There's always a problem with the client relationship—you just don't know what it is."

Anticipate the nasty surprises

Start with your risk spreadsheet from Rule 26. Might your biggest customer go bankrupt? Might your best engineer jump to the competition? Might your supplier become a competitor?

The biggest surprises for your team are likely to erupt close to home. As happened to one of my interviewees two months into his new role, engineering altered their plans and, oops, forgot to involve marketing in mapping the implications.

Andy Grove, when CEO of Intel, famously worried about noticing "strategic inflection points"—when the fundamentals of your market change.[27] If ever you start to think of your market, technology, or channels as fairly stable, catch yourself.

Let your team see you ask hard questions

Ask questions that cultivate healthy paranoia and lead to good business decisions:

- How do we know that?
- What would be a sign that we're wrong?
- What if that's true, yet for part of the market, the opposite is true?
- If new entrants wanted to shake up this market, what might they do?
- Whose expertise could give us a different view of this?

---

27. Andrew Grove, *Only the Paranoid Survive*, 1 ed. (New York, NY: Doubleday Business, 1996).

But shouldn't you stay upbeat to build morale?

No! Ignoring potential landmines makes you dead, not upbeat.

I did say "healthy" paranoia, and this is what I mean: Your team becomes focused and energized as they hunt for early signals of change, not depressed and anxious. They know they have the smarts, routines, and tools to notice when things change, figure out which changes matter, adapt their plans, and rally resources.

You build morale by giving people the experience of doing something, succeeding, and seeing the link between their actions and that success. So, look for opportunities to coach your team through investigating reality and adapting as needed.

Be aware of competing agendas

The guy running marketing wants you to succeed as head of sales because he's compensated in part on revenue. He knows if you're effective in herding the cats in the field, his team members will find it easier to roll out initiatives. Furthermore, he generally supports the collaborative culture the executive team has maintained. At the same time, he'd prefer your star to shine a little less brightly than his own. He knows the CEO is considering implementing a business unit structure as the company grows, and he'd like to remain the top choice to head up mobile products.

You can figure any two people in your organization have agendas that compete. Given this reality, people (including you and your team members) take actions sometimes to advance a personal agenda over the best interests of the organization or fellow team members. (That's why extending trust and being worthy of trust are such valued currencies.)

Notice early when you are in the crosshairs and take wise action. Jeffrey Pfeffer describes in Power, "If you don't stand up for yourself and actively promote your own interests, few will be willing to be on your side."[28]

Be most wary of yourself

Just stepping into a position called "executive" or "manager" messes with your mind. Excellent social psychology research shows that seeing yourself in a powerful position relative to your immediate group makes you more susceptible to buying your own initial interpretation of the situation.[29]

The higher you go, the harder you must work to become aware of and challenge your own reasoning. So, form some trusted relationships with people who will kick-test your thoughts, engage an executive coach who understands strategy, and—most importantly—create a safe atmosphere and frequent opportunity for your team to challenge you and each other.

---

28. Jeffrey Pfeffer, *Power: Why Some People Have It—and Others Don't*, San Francisco, CA, Jossey-Bass, 2000).
29. Adam D. Galinsky et al, "Power and Perspectives Not Taken," *Psychological Science* 17, no. 12 (2006): 1068–1074.

35

Ferret Out Feedback

Leaders need more feedback than ever—and they're less likely to get it. You need more feedback because chances are you're doing what used to be two or three jobs. Regional sales VPs are now also running channel partnerships. The office manager is somehow also covering the accounts payable vacancy. You don't even know what you don't know about some of your responsibilities. Plus, with your market environment in flux, hard decisions are coming your way faster than ever.

However, you're even less likely to hear feedback up, down, or sideways. You can't count on informal feedback, as many people fear annoying anyone in power. You may not even receive formal feedback, as review cycles are disrupted by job changes—including yours.

Figure out what you want to know

You may want to know whether the exec team is sitting on your product development recommendations because they're waiting for a market signal or because they don't trust your data. You want to know whether those silent nods at the end of meetings means your team members agree and are rushing off to go implement, or they're confused by what you said and are awaiting more clear direction. You want to know if the subject matter expert two levels below and one across believes you're about to wade into an avoidable mess.

Forge your own feedback channels
- Ask.
  "What am I doing that's helping you accomplish X?" "When am I a roadblock to you and your team?" "How might I screw this up?" "What issues or people should I be giving more attention?"

The higher up you are, the more you have to ask for it. Talk to people in functions upstream and downstream to what you do. Ask your boss and others, "let me know if you hear from others things that could help me be more effective."

*   Initiate it yourself.
    Don't wait for an annual process to receive upward feedback. If you can't hire an executive coach, arrange for a trusted peer to interview your team and summarize key messages back up.
*   Respond tremendously well.
    Fastest way to kill your feedback channel: downplay the feedback, even slightly, verbally or non-verbally. (See the online resources for this Rule for my simple chart on how to respond well to feedback.)
*   Make sure your team members are also getting feedback—from you and others across your organization. Ask them what feedback channels they've put in place for themselves, how they're using the feedback, and what you can do to support their learning. By showing your appetite for hearing feedback and using it well, you shift your company's culture from "pretending I know it all" toward "let's learn how to be more and more successful."

Ask for the good stuff

You're tough, right? You want the "hard stuff." You can handle the bad news about your weaknesses. Good, because you need to know when your well-intentioned behavior is having a negative impact. Just don't stop there.

Turns out our brains learn best from successes, not failures.[30] This is especially true when the feedback about success comes soon after the win. So don't wait to let a team member know that you saw brilliance in how s/he just resolved a brewing argument between two execs. Says OD strategist Bart Fisher, "When you're doing what comes naturally, sometimes you don't see how powerful that strength really is."

Same for you—you want to train your brain to recognize and learn from success. Some of this you can do yourself—make a habit of scanning each performance-testing situation for success. Some successes are best described by the team. Ask, "What did we do well? What can we learn from this?"

---

30. Deborah Halber. "MIT News: Why We Learn More From our Successes than our Failures." July 29, 2009,
http://web.mit.edu/newsoffice/2009/successes-0729.html

36 Build Your Industry Presence

Wouldn't you rather work for someone well-networked and industry-savvy than a super-great boss who focuses only on his or her team?

Your investment in increasing your external profile can strengthen your own team's commitment. Plus, building your personal brand will also expand possibilities for your next role. External visibility often increases promotion opportunities and compensation leverage, as well as making you visible to other companies.

Set your goals

As examples, here's what some of my contacts aim to accomplish:

- Earn a reputation for savvy public speaking that raises his chances of securing a CFO role (corporate controller)
- Bridge from her consumer packaged goods expertise to a career shift to online marketing (marketing director)
- Become sufficiently visible that she's the first call when regional companies need guidance (crisis management consultant)
- Hear about industry and policy developments faster than anyone else in the company, so she can make wise strategic recommendations and move up (product marketing manager)

Craft your presence growth strategy

Consider a sequence of growth that will work well for you. For example, you might use a blog and Twitter to establish yourself as a valuable contributor on an aspect of your industry. Then, speak to several small groups to hone a distinct message, prepare an eBook or company white paper, and lead workshops externally and perhaps internally. Make some deliberate moves now, and adjust as you learn.

Since there are so many ways to get out there, pick ones you enjoy!

If you enjoy writing, start or contribute to a blog. Family commitments make it hard to show up for local networking cocktails? You can podcast and write articles after kids are in bed. Enjoy speaking? Master the art of the conference proposal...then if you're good, conference organizers will come to you.

Challenge yourself to increase value-for-time

Treat your time in social media, industry breakfasts, etc., like any other investment. You can't afford to lose hours Twittering aimlessly. Drive toward exceptional value for time, and drop the low-yield activities.

Learn from the experts. The *42 Rules* catalog includes expert guidance on using social media for business and building your presence on LinkedIn.

Build 1-1 relationships, face-to-face when possible. Humans are wired to build trust through face-to-face interactions. Skype and phone are imperfect substitutes, and email-to-email is even less useful for building trust.[31]

Use networking sites and email lists as ways to find people consistent with your goals, and then, after positive online interactions, arrange a call or meeting. Arranging to meet people with whom you've formed a virtual connection is also a terrific way to realize value from conferences.

Guide your team in building their presence

Many leaders are unaware or reactive about what their team members are doing for online or face-to-face networking. While you can't control their actions, you can guide team members in building their presence:

- Create industry presence goals with your group; map specific people to cover desired info channels, areas of expertise, etc.
- Make industry presence part of your conversation with each team member about goals in current role and preparation for the next.
- Mentor team members in building skills, expertise, and networks to succeed in accomplishing their goals. As with yourself, encourage activities that draw on their strengths and also recognize when they need to shore up or work around relevant weaknesses. If you've got someone who's a great speaker, give them opportunities to master that craft.
- If protecting intellectual property is important to your group, work with your team (and legal) to craft ground rules that protect the business, while giving your people enough room to offer meaningful content.

---

31. Kevin W. Rockmanna and Gregory B. Northcraft, "To be or not to be Trusted," *Organizational Behavior and Human Decision Processes* 107, no. 2 (2008): 106–122.

Part VII
Set You and Your Team To Thrive

How long do you want to do this work of leadership? What do you hope to accomplish?

Many people can drive themselves and their teams to exceed expectations for a quarter or two. The real challenge is to build a team—and a life—that sustains high performance. And, to know, at the end of some very long days, that your hard work was worth it.

Read this section for the refinements that separate superb leaders from the so-so, and balanced careers from burnouts.

- Rule 37: Make Your Job Doable
- Rule 38: Stoke the Energy of Your Group
- Rule 39: Mind Your Mood
- Rule 40: Now, Lead with Your Life in Mind
- Rule 41: Use Your Power for Good
- Rule 42: These Are My Rules. What Are Yours?

Make Your Job Doable

Very few people thoughtfully manage the scope of their job. I suggest you do.

Reframe the criteria for success

There's no shortage of ways to view your job. At a minimum, there's what you think you're supposed to be doing, what your boss thinks, what your team thinks, and your by-now-buried job description. Chances are, these four views of your job are all different. Even worse, none of them may be doable.

You want to be evaluated on a short, relevant set of metrics. Refine your criteria to the critical three to five priorities, and then align expectations for what you will deliver.

While you'll find more flexibility in small and mid-sized companies, mid-level leaders in larger companies can sometimes alter formal company metrics. In any case, you can definitely use metrics to drive the off-P&L understanding of your function.

Organize your priorities

Let's start by considering what leaders do:
- Set direction (strategizing, planning)
- Engage and mobilize people (developing, communicating)
- Enable execution (hiring, budgeting, coordinating)
- Other stuff only you do

I offer the first three buckets with thanks to Sharon Richmond, now Director of Cisco's Change Leadership Center of Excellence, and my co-author on leadership research. Sharon developed this simple yet powerful model of what leaders do.[32] The fourth bucket reflects the reality that many leaders have an "individual contributor" component to their job.

For each of these buckets, note the priority responsibilities of this job. Said an executive I interviewed: "You can only really care about three things at a time, maybe five." Note what you think you should be doing (how many hours per month you'd allocate to each, to maximize business results). Finally, leave yourself some time to participate, lead, or initiate cross-functional efforts that drive value to a broader P&L.

Then note other initiatives that take significant time, but either don't fall into these buckets or aren't priorities for you. "When you find an individual opportunity, hand it down with your mentoring," says Pat Arensdorf, CEO of Critical Diagnostics. "You can't do many of those yourself. Turn most over to your team."

Laying out your priorities in an organized way prepares you to have a conversation with your boss, coach, and others who can help you redesign your job and re-set expectations to line up with value for the business.

Deflect early requests to go off-mission

Especially in small companies or recession-decimated larger ones there tend to be too few bodies, which leads to many requests to take on extraneous tasks. While some of these "yanks" are non-negotiable, saying yes will derail you from bigger goals. Again from Pat Arensdorf: "You can be a hero by clearing the plate a bit but beware: you might be successful and this might become expected, and you may never get to what you were hired to do."

Another challenge arises for new leaders from underrepresented populations. "Finally! A Latina on a divisional exec team! Let's get her in the mentoring program." "Finally! Someone in product design with a materials engineering background. Let's pull him onto the green team." Etc. Totally understandable. And, if this is you, you're in for some tough but valuable conversations about when would be the right time for you to add which of these activities.

---

32. Sharon L. Richmond. *Introduction to Type & Leadership: Develop more effective leaders of every type*, (Mountain View, CA: CPP, 2008).

38 Stoke the Energy of Your Group

"Go on the hunt for metrics exceeded, customers delighted, missteps avoided, and problems solved."

Congrats! You've got the right people on your team, doing the right things. Now how are you going to keep them, and keep them productive?

Manage the pressure cooker

It's up to you to translate organizational expectations so your team stays bold rather than burned-out.

- Be thoughtful about which stressors to let roll to your team and which stop with you.
- When team members have been kicking it hard, give them some downtime, in ways that are meaningful to them (such as, feel free to take off the day of your choice next week).
- Set the tone that we're experimenting and learning.
- Communicate in ways that are genuine and human. Watch your subtle cues that signal whether "it's OK here" to show real reactions, or whether reactions have to stay bottled up.

Remember: Brains like wins

Research in progress from my colleague Dr. Dario Nardi of UCLA shows that brains go into "flow" pattern when people "win" something.[33] This is true even if the win is in a kid's card game based mostly on luck. Brains like wins.

So, call attention to wins. Celebrate wins. Heck, engineer some wins. Go on the hunt for metrics exceeded, customers delighted, missteps avoided, and problems solved. Find real reasons for your team to feel successful.

---

33. http://www.darionardi.com/articles.html

Focus on the middle performers who could be even better

That's a conclusion of recent research on 200,000 360° feedback reports by Jack Zenger, et al.[34] "In short, we've been putting our leadership development emphasis on the wrong populations. Rather than focus on the top end or the bottom end, our efforts should be directed to the large group in the middle. Building these good leaders' capability to behave like top-tier leaders can produce results that are far beyond incremental."

I see too many leaders spend the bulk of their time prodding C players and pal-ing around with A players. Your A players probably need less of your time, and your C players should either prove they can step up to B or go. Coach your B players, and some will become A. Others will simply be great, hardworking, productive members of your team. Fine.

Don't race too far ahead of your team

We admire leaders who set high standards, right? Who do everything in their power to "model the way" by driving hard themselves?

This "Pacesetting" leadership style sounds great, until you do it. Moving faster than your team feeds a cycle that destroys morale, squashes initiative, stunts skill development, and keeps you working weekends. In a study by Goleman, this style nearly tied with a coercive style for negative impact on organizational performance.[35] Instead of racing around hoping your team will follow, set clear performance targets with all your team members and see what they need from you to accomplish the targets.

Transform complaints to commitments

Underneath every complaint is a commitment.[36] When salespeople complain about Legal, they're committed to making sales—to their benefit and the company's. When Legal complains about Sales, often they're committed to protecting the company from excessive risk.

You can show your team members how to identify their own commitments. Note that I did not say they have to identify a solution. Leaders who insist that anyone who mentions a problem provide a solution soon find they don't hear about many problems. Conversely, you may hear your team members offering solutions without thinking through the problem; use questions to point them back to problem definition.

When your team talks more about their commitments than their complaints, you'll find they partner far more effectively with others inside and outside the team.

---

34. Jack Zenger et al. "Five Insights From Leadership Research," July, 2009, http://www.workforce.com/section/11/feature/26/52/35/index_printer.html
35. Daniel Goleman, "Leadership that Gets Results," *Harvard Business Review*, March/April 2000, 78–90.
36. Robert Kegan and Lisa Lahey Laskow, *How the Way We Talk Can Change the Way We Work: Seven Languages for Transformation*, 1st ed. (San Francisco, CA: Jossey-Bass, 2002).

Mind Your Mood

"Cultivate the wisdom to notice that most unwelcome events don't mean total disaster."

When you add more stress, do you become more productive? A little bit of stress can improve performance by making you alert, excited, ready to act. However, most people become less productive and less creative under even moderate mental stress. Psychologists use "threat rigidity" to describe the diminishment of original, flexible, productive thought under conditions of stress.

If you're feeling rigid and panicky, your team will pick up on this. Humans are wired to absorb each other's moods in what's called "emotional contagion." If you're feeling confident in your ability to handle what comes, your team will often mirror this sense of calm.

Keep your cool

Some people try to keep their cool by aiming to hide their panic, anger, or annoyance. This "expressive suppression" seldom works.

Instead, choose to look at situations more flexibly, so you genuinely feel more optimistic and capable. Cultivate the wisdom to notice that most unwelcome events don't mean total disaster. Cognitive framing—how you describe the situation to yourself—is your most important lever for remaining calm and constructive.

Expect to be "hijacked" and practice your resets

- Clue in to your early warning systems
  Often our bodies offer us clues that we're hooked. Perhaps your gut twists every time you try to act like you've got it all together when really it's time to ask for help. Or, your shoulders tighten when

you slip into your skeptical "prove you're not out to get me" stance. You can use these clues to notice you've jumped into a pattern.

- Become familiar with what you do under stress
  A set of learnings called the Enneagram is the best roadmap I've seen for understanding deep personal patterns...patterns so ingrained that expecting us to see them on our own is truly like asking fish to describe water. See if the Enneagram offers you some fresh insight into your habitual behaviors and underlying beliefs. (See Appendix D.)
- Consider your choices and re-train your triggers
  If you have a pattern, for example, of reacting to ambiguity with aggressive moves to control the situation, what other choices might you make? Can you learn to recognize the situations that trigger patterns you'd like to adjust?
- Cultivate calm in your life
  Our defensive patterns are most likely to run the show when we're stressed, overwhelmed, and tired. Consider what you can do to cultivate a "relaxation response" rather than "flight, fight, or freeze." Even two minutes of intentional calm in the middle of a frenzied day might be a real help in noticing your patterns and choosing actions that will serve you.

Build the body of a leader

Have you ever noticed the arms of a waitress? Strong. The torso of a mountain climber? Flexible. The legs of a surgeon? Steady. The neck of a pianist? Relaxed.

We seldom think about it, but leaders have bodies, too. What their bodies do becomes amplified across their teams. When a leader has tense, irregular breathing that often transmits stress to a team. When a leader has stiff posture, people form an impression of interpersonal rigidity. When a leader fidgets, others wonder whether he or she is confident and committed.

What kind of body will support you in being a leader in your environment? What sort of strength, flexibility, endurance, relaxation will enable you to lead with effectiveness and ease?

Get sleep

Executive energy expert Tony Schwartz, "Great performers sleep one to two hours a night more than others."[37] If you think you're the special one who can do fine on six hours or less, you're probably kidding yourself. At least, test it. See what happens to the quality of your thinking with an extra hour of sleep each night.

---

37. Wayne Turmel. "The Cranky Middle Manager Show #244 The Way we're Working Isn't Working Tony Schwartz," July 6, 2010. http://cmm.thepodcastnetwork.com/2010/07/06/the-cranky-mid-dle-manager-show-244-the-way-were-working-isnt-work-ing-tony-schwartz/

40 Now, Lead with Your Life in Mind

"It's up to you to clear the decks."

There's no down season in leadership anymore. Stop waiting for quiet periods between major initiatives, and design your life to be sane nearly every day.

Figure out what you need to be a happy mammal

Sunshine? Feasting with friends? Walks alone outside? Fulfilling companionship? Sleep?

It's easy to forget that underneath the fancy clothes and cell phones, we're primates who not so long ago were picking berries off bushes. Our lifestyles have changed, but our core needs remain.

You can ignore your own needs for sleep, sunshine, and snuggling for brief periods of urgent work. Of course, if you push until you break, then break you will, with lousy consequences for all.

If "crisis mode" has become your daily MO, schedule an appointment with yourself or a good friend to figure out a more sustainable way to manage your work and life.

And, offer the same flexibility for your staff, whenever possible. One of my interviewees had three full-time direct reports: one who arrived at 9 AM after working out each morning; another who left at 2:30 to pick-up her kids; and another who front-loaded work so he could take planned days out each month for shifts at a local urgent care to maintain his clinical skills. As John Medina describes in his readable book *Brain Rules*, when people are satisfied with their lives, they are more productive at work.[38] Create an environment in which your team members thrive as people, and you set yourself up for high performance.

Take mastery of your calendar

Shared access to Outlook has fostered the ridiculous notion that everyone else is in charge of your day. They're not. You are.

Typically, the higher you go, the more control you have over your calendar. Exercise that control. Set aside time on your calendar for tasks you have to complete. Others won't know if that block marked "busy" means "preparing a crucial presentation for investors" (of course they wouldn't interrupt) or "thinking" (you know they would).

Help your team figure out when to communicate with you. If you need long stretches of uninterrupted time, let them know.

Create days and weeks and years that work

Do your best thinking at morning or night? By yourself or with others?

Know yourself, and set up systems that make the most of your time.

If you're a morning person, tackle the challenging tasks first and complete less-demanding work at the end of the day. If you're a slower starter, ease in with the hum-drum and use the afternoons for tasks that require a brain firing on all cylinders.

If there's a time of year when your business usually is slower—the first quarter, for example, if you're in retail—make sure you tackle long-term projects or strategic thinking during those months. That way, they'll be less likely to fall victim to the tyranny of the urgent.

Gain energy from purpose

What do you want to experience in the time you're on the planet? Love? Peace? Leading a truly great company? Adrenaline rushes? Six decades of golf? Sweet toddler kisses? Winters at the cabin with your clan?

Other people will not schedule this on your calendar. It's up to you to clear the decks to allow time to clear your head. Take those non-work goals and translate them into real-world activities—daily exercise, quarterly vacations, whatever. Now, put them in your calendar! I know this sounds basic—have you done it yet?

---

38. John Medina. *Brain Rules: 12 Principles for Surviving and Thriving at Work, Home, and School* (Seattle, WA: Pear Press, 2008).

Use Your Power for Good

Most leaders reach a point where they ask, "Why am I working so hard, beyond making money?"

What do you want to make happen in the world?

- Prove that a small company can transform your industry?
- Close the digital divide?
- Create pedestrian-friendly cities?
- Make rockin' awesome products?
- Help dads be more involved with their kids?
- Bring high-end science to low-income schools?

Your work will inevitably have some impact on the lives of your team members with ripples through your community and even the world. Amplify that impact by clarifying your intentions and focusing your actions.

Inventory ways to use your power

- Offer your personal example
- Encourage and mentor others
- Introduce people who can do good together
- Help reshape company policy
- Offer access for research
- Redirect company investments of time or money
- Write or speak about non-proprietary practices that have broader value
- Share your methodology with a nonprofit
- Start or lead cross-sector or community initiatives

Nudge your organization forward

As Stanford Professor Debra Meyerson showed in her book *Tempered Radicals*, you can rock the boat yet stay on board.[39] If you're willing to be both courageous and patient, you can make change while maintaining professional credibility. Be positive—and persistent—in building support for changes that matter to you, whether choosing green suppliers or mentoring diverse candidates into senior roles.

You can make positive change happen at any point in your career. Take advantage of corporate-wide social media—which lowers the cost of organizing and gives voice to people at any career stage—and expansion of corporate social responsibility priorities from the top. Look for company priorities that match your personal goals and offer to lead initiatives.

Launch something audacious

Tom Tierney, Chairman of the strategy consultancy Bain & Company and head of the Bain SF office when I started my career there, described in an inspiring Stanford interview that he considered for years the difference he wanted to make.[40] He decided to launch Bridgespan, a nonprofit consulting group filling a critical gap in supporting nonprofit leadership and strategy. Another Bain alum, Lindsay Levin, answered that question of contribution by founding Leaders'Quest, an amazing organization guiding executives on experiential journeys in fast-changing parts of the world, and developing emerging leaders in resource-challenged communities.[41]

Come back to what matters to you

As you progress through your leadership career, you'll find plenty of causes eager for your counsel and even more eager for your access, influence, and funding. As McKinsey partner Bill Meehan put it, "Demand for my time at the price of zero is infinite."

Rather than passively respond to requests you receive, scan for (or create) opportunities that matter to you. John A. Byrne, former Editor-in-Chief of FastCompany and BusinessWeek.com, encourages MBAs visiting his new venture, Poets&Quants, to "embrace who you are and your dreams...look inside your soul and decide what you really want to do with your life."[42]

Just as you've developed a strategy for achieving your on-the-job goals, come up with a plan for other changes you want to foster. You can't tackle everything as a leader, and you can't accomplish everything as a change agent either. Decide what changes have meaning for you, and go for it!

---

39. Debra E Meyerson, *Tempered Radicals*, 1st ed. (Boston, MA: Harvard Business School Press, 2003).
40. Tom Tierney, "Social Innovation Conversations: Nonprofit Management and the Leadership Deficit," January 18, 2007, http://sic.conversationsnetwork.org/shows/detail3213.html
41. Lindsay Levin, "Leaders' Quest: Connecting and Inspiring Leaders Around the World," http://www.leadersquest.org/
42. Pam Fox Rollin. "Weekly Leader Podcast Episode 63 | John A. Byrne, Poets & Quants," http://weeklyleader.net/2010/weekly-leader-podcast-episode-63-john-a-byrne-poets-quants-part-2/

42

These Are My Rules. What Are Yours?

I've coached and spoken with thousands of new and experienced leaders, and I've interviewed dozens of successful executives specifically for this book. Their experiences are the basis for this book, and I'm grateful to each one of them.

Now this work of helping others succeed moves from their voice to yours.

As you hire new leaders for your own team, what do you see them do to make a strong start? What actions are working for them, and what actions are causing them to stumble?

Extend a hand to the next round of leaders by sharing what you've learned. I've created a blog to make this easy (http://ideashape.com/link/addyourrule). There you can add your insights to the rules in this book and post rules of your own.

I'm also glad to connect with you on Twitter @Lead-StartBook and @PamFR. If you'd prefer to share your experiences or ask questions privately, feel free to email me book@ideashape.com.

Wishing you huge success, tremendous satisfaction, and great fun along the way!

A For Job Seekers

"Succeed before you start."

Make an even stronger start by taking advantage of these rules before you say "yes" to the job.

How to use this book now:

- **Rock your interviews**
  Draft your strategic point of view before you interview—see Rule #4. Use Rules #6 through #10 to ask better questions about how this team creates business value, what's at stake, what the team is expected to and could accomplish, and metrics the company is using and could use for this team. Let Rules #11 through #13 guide how you describe your strengths and weaknesses and how you position your experience.

- **Decide which job offer presents more opportunity**
  To accelerate your career growth, you want to lead groups that have the potential to deliver extraordinary value. See Rules #6 through #10 to sharpen your analysis of which job you want to take.

- **Negotiate your start**
  Read Rules #4, #5, and #6 to figure out what you want to have in place before Day 1. Then come back to Rule #2 and time your start.

- **Take best advantage of time between hire and start**
  Whether you're being promoted or hired in from outside the company, the time between receiving an offer and starting your role is gold. See Rules #2 and #6 to use that time well.

- **Succeed from Day 1**
  You've reached for this book because you see that the difference between a mediocre start and a strong start is HUGE. There's no better time than now to initiate critical relationships, define who you are, set goals, decide where to invest your time, and start creating wins. This book gives you powerful areas to focus on when creating your own plan for success right from the start.
- **Make future roles come to you**
  As you apply the guidance in this book, along with your own wisdom and hard work, you'll build a record of success. You'll also build a network of engaged team members, impressed peers, and valued executive relationships. Your track record and network can bring the next opportunities right to you.

All my best for your job search! Keep in touch and let me know how you made your smart start.

B Hiring? How to Use this Book

How many days are you spending each month coaching, making performance plans for, and cleaning up after your high potential but underperforming managers, directors, and VPs?

If you're like many business unit heads, the answer is two to four days per month—that's 10 to 20 percent of your time. If you're an HR business partner, you could easily be spending 25 to 40 percent of your time on people who have everything it takes to succeed yet aren't succeeding.

Most importantly, how many of those leaders would be on a better trajectory had they made a stronger start? My interviewees figure roughly 25 to 50 percent.

The returns are enormous on helping your new leaders start well. So what can you do?

- **Give your hires time to start**
  Before you tell new hires to start next Monday, consider the benefit of having them start rested and well. Especially if they're being promoted from within, see if you can give them time to make a strong close on their old role plus rest up.
- **Make onboarding programs worth their time**
  Give each leadership hire and promote access to a smart, high-value standard set of onboarding activities and also a custom path coordinated with his/her boss. Give hires maximum flexibility by using videos/texts on demand and keeping cattle call sessions to a minimum. Do keep face-to-face interaction when valuable, typically strategy and culture conversations with senior executives, plus peer networking.

- **Kick start the conversation**
  Instead of tacitly encouraging new leaders to act as if they know what's going on, hook them up with helpful people right from the beginning. For front-line managers, this may take the form of "start buddies" a level or two higher. For executives, sometimes the best guide to company culture is a peer or even one step down with experience in different functions. Pick guides who are known to be trustworthy and effective in the company.
- **Give new hires—and their bosses—this book**
  Your investment in giving this book to each of your new hires will save you hours of mentoring time and could earn your business hundreds of thousands of dollars by making each new leadership hire more successful.

C For Executive Coaches

"Support your
client's success,
right from the
start."

When was the last time **you** started a new job, evaluated the team you were handed, negotiated targets with a new boss, and figured out how to navigate a new peer group and complex organization?

If you're like many executive coaches I know, it's been a while since you were in the trenches.

Use this book to put your head back in the game.

- **Remind yourself of the challenges your clients are facing**
  Skim the book and dive into the issues most relevant to your clients.
- **Contribute to the coaching agenda**
  What issues might be important for your clients to address now? In three months? In six months? Pick several rules that you believe will have value for each of your clients and point them towards those learnings.
- **Offer this book as a blueprint**
  Talk through the Rules together, and help your clients customize the guidance for their specific situations.
- **Coach your clients to step up to the challenges**
  Which Rules do they disagree with or find daunting? How can they tackle these situations in ways that work for them?

- **Help your clients be aware of who they are "being" as well as what they are "doing"**
  Some task-oriented types become so focused on milestones and tactics that they under-use the power of "showing up" with clarity, curiosity, compassion, and commitment. See especially Rules #6, #13, and #20–23. You can help them step up to this part of leadership. In so doing, you'll accelerate their leadership career in a way no task list can.

I want this book to be a powerful tool for your coaching. Feel free to get in touch with me to talk through any of this.

D Myers-Briggs® and More

As busy as leaders are in those first few months, many find value in assessments such as the Myers-Briggs Type Indicator® (MBTI®). Assessments, and the models that underlie them, give you language for what you see in yourself, the new job, and your workplace. When you're moving fast, and the stakes are high, you want powerful and easy-to-digest ways to increase your insight.

In your first few months you may use assessments for these purposes:

- **Profile the job and define your strengths and stretches**
  Assessments such as the MBTI® and the StrengthsFinder® can remind you of areas of strength for you to leverage in your new role. Some assessments, including the Kolbe Index®, have materials specifically designed to help you diagnose the job, identify how your profile matches up to the role, and how you may adapt to those stretches. See Rules #11 and #12 for guidance on applying strengths and weaknesses as you start a new leadership role.

- **Bring awareness to your blindspots**
  Each of us has aspects of our behavior and impact about which we are rather unaware. My clients have found tremendous value in both the MBTI® and the Enneagram, as offered via assessments such as the Breckenridge Type Indicator®.

- **Build relationships and be effective with other styles**
  Many of these models include descriptions of other styles. Review this material when you find yourself frustrated with or perplexed by a co-worker with whom you'd like to be more effective. You'll probably discover that person

would make a lousy version of you, yet a most excellent version of him/herself that could potentially be quite effective in his/her own way. You'll find MBTI® and other assessments useful in building relationships as you work through Rules #6, #15, #27, #28, and #30.

- **Diagnose the culture and your team**
  Your first few months are seldom a good time to launch formal assessments of organizational culture and team functioning. However, you can gain insight into your team by thinking through the frameworks underlying diagnostics such as those from The Table Group. Use these frameworks to guide your curiosity about what aspects of your organization are helping or hindering performance.

While you'll gain the most value by working with an expert coach or facilitator, you can introduce yourself to the models through books or videos. Visit this book's website for links to these assessments and related resources (http://ideashape.com/link/assessments).

Online Resources

"Keep learning as you succeed in this role...and your next!"

This book is your gateway to ever-expanding content to help you succeed in this leadership role...and the next.

You'll find links to all the extra content mentioned in this book online at (http://ideashape.com/leadstartbook/resources). Resources include worksheet templates, other materials I've created for you, and links to great content on other sites.

And, look for "Add your own rule" (http://ideashape.com/link/addyourrule) to share your hard-won lessons!

Author

About the Author

Photo credit: Lifestyles Imaging

Pam Fox Rollin coaches executives to succeed in broader roles and guides senior teams to make the most of new talent. Pam is known as a dynamic speaker and valuable thought-partner to leaders navigating themselves and their organizations through complex change. Pam's company, IdeaShape Coaching & Consulting, also facilitates strategy sessions, Myers-Briggs® team-building, and leadership offsites. Clients include Genentech/Roche, Accenture, Autodesk and other top companies in biotech, consulting, and technology. Her MBA is from Stanford University's Graduate School of Business, where she later served as a Guest Fellow and Master Coach.

Write Your Own Rules

You can write your own 42 Rules book, and we can help you do it—from initial concept, to writing and editing, to publishing and marketing. If you have a great idea for a 42 Rules book, then we want to hear from you.

As you know, the books in the 42 Rules series are practical guidebooks that focus on a single topic. The books are written in an easy-to-read format that condenses the fundamental elements of the topic into 42 Rules. They use realistic examples to make their point and are fun to read.

Two Kinds of 42 Rules Books

42 Rules books are published in two formats: the single-author book and the contributed-author book. The single-author book is a traditional book written by one author. The contributed-author book (like *42 Rules for Working Moms*) is a compilation of Rules, each written by a different contributor, which support the main topic. If you want to be the sole author of a book or one of its contributors, we can help you succeed!

42 Rules Program

A lot of people would like to write a book, but only a few actually do. Finding a publisher, and distributing and marketing the book are challenges that prevent even the most ambitious of authors to ever get started.

At 42 Rules, we help you focus on and be successful in the writing of your book. Our program concentrates on the following tasks so you don't have to.

- **Publishing:** You receive expert advice and guidance from the Executive Editor, copy editors, technical editors, and cover and layout designers to help you create your book.

- **Distribution:** We distribute your book through the major book distribution channels, like Baker and Taylor and Ingram, Amazon.com, Barnes and Noble, Borders Books, etc.

- **Marketing:** 42 Rules has a full-service marketing program that includes a customized Web page for you and your book, email registrations and campaigns, blogs, webcasts, media kits and more.

Whether you are writing a single-authored book or a contributed-author book, you will receive editorial support from 42 Rules Executive Editor, Laura Lowell, author of *42 Rules of Marketing*, which was rated Top 5 in Business Humor and Top 25 in Business Marketing on Amazon.com (December 2007), and author and Executive Editor of *42 Rules for Working Moms*.

Accepting Submissions

If you want to be a successful author, we'll provide you the tools to help make it happen. Start today by answering the following questions and visit our website at http://superstarpress.com/ for more information on submitting your 42 Rules book idea.

Super Star Press is now accepting submissions for books in the 42 Rules book series. For more information, email info@superstarpress.com or call 408-257-3000.

Other Happy About Books

42 Rules for Growing Enterprise Revenue

This book is a brainstorming tool meant to provoke discussion and creativity within executive teams who are looking to boost their top line numbers.

Paperback: $19.95
eBook: $14.95

42 Rules for Creating WE

42 Rules for Creating WE offers new insights from thought leaders in neuroscience, organizational development, and brand strategy, introducing groundbreaking practices for bringing the spirit of WE to any organization, team or cause.

Paperback: $19.95
eBook: $14.95

Scrappy Women in Business

This refreshingly honest book provides welcome reassurance for every businesswoman who's ever wondered, "Is it me, or has the whole rest of the company gone nuts?!"

Paperback: $19.95
eBook: $14.95

42 Rules of Employee Engagement

This book is loaded with practical advice and actions you can take away to begin building an engaged team.

Paperback: $19.95
eBook: $14.95

Purchase these books at Happy About
http://happyabout.com/
or at other online and physical bookstores.

A Message From Super Star Press™

Thank you for your purchase of this 42 Rules Series book. It is available online at: http://www.happyabout.com/42rules/yournewleadershiprole.php or at other online and physical bookstores. To learn more about contributing to books in the 42 Rules series, check out http://superstarpress.com.

Please contact us for quantity discounts at sales@superstarpress.com.

If you want to be informed by email of upcoming books, please email bookupdate@superstarpress.com.

CPSIA information can be obtained at www.ICGtesting.com
Printed in the USA
265710BV00004B/1/P